Legal and Ethical Considerations for Public Relations

Second Edition

Karla K. Gower
University of Alabama

WAVELAND

PRESS, INC.

Long Grove, Illinois

For information about this book, contact:
Waveland Press, Inc.
4180 IL Route 83, Suite 101
Long Grove, IL 60047-9580
(847) 634-0081
info@waveland.com
www.waveland.com

CONTENTS

iv   Contents

PREFACE

Law is an instrument of social control that regulates human behavior. It is both prohibitory (one must not steal) and mandatory (one must wear seat belts). The primary function of law is to maintain stability in the social, political, and economic system, while at the same time permitting peaceful change. It serves its primary function by resolving disputes, protecting property, and preserving the state.[1]

Because law reflects a society's values, norms, and beliefs, it is affected by morals. But morals, or ethics, and the law are not the same. Ethics is the study of what constitutes right or wrong behavior. It attempts to determine what people ought to do in a situation, not what they are legally required to do or prevented from doing. For example, a public relations professional is not legally required to answer a reporter's questions that go beyond the information contained in a news release but may feel an ethical obligation to do so. Legal responsibilities can be seen as setting minimum standards for behavior that society is willing to tolerate, while ethical obligations may well require higher standards or in some cases different standards. The death penalty is legal in most states, for example, but many see it as an unethical form of punishment.

Public relations professionals need an understanding of both law and ethics. Knowledge of one without the other is not sufficient. The public relations professional's failure to know the law can expose the professional and the organization to liability, but so can failing to do the "right thing." An organization's publics can suffer harm from breaches of ethical duties, ultimately resulting in harm to the organization. Yet, studies suggest that public relations professionals are deficient in knowledge in both areas.

A study of business ethics programs, for example, has revealed that public relations professionals are not key players in the corporate ethics process despite the fact that public relations is often described as the conscience of an organization. A number of factors may cause corporations not to look to public relations professionals for ethical guidance, but certainly one factor would appear to be a lack of understanding of ethics on the part of management and public relations professionals. An increased knowledge of ethics, then, can help public relations professionals educate management on the ethical consequences of corporate action.

Similarly, a study of public relations professionals revealed that they consider themselves only somewhat familiar with the law despite its serious implications for organizations.[2] As attorney Morton Simon put it, "They can and have cost companies millions of dollars. They have contributed toward litigation. They have helped companies lose valuable trademarks. They have resulted in charges of unfair labor practices. They have led to Securities and Exchange Commission (SEC) problems. The catalogue is almost endless."[3]

Nor do public relations practitioners appear to have an accurate view of lawyers and their attitudes toward the importance of public opinion. Lawyers, on the other hand, "have a fairly accurate view of public relations counselors," according to one study.[4] This failure on the part of public relations professionals to understand lawyers makes it difficult for the two groups to resolve corporate crises collaboratively.

Despite the importance of understanding law and ethics for public relations professionals, few works address law and ethics from a public relations perspective. Most books on mass communication law focus on the law as it affects journalists. Although helpful for public relations professionals, these works either gloss over issues of importance to public relations or ignore them altogether. This book discusses the important legal and ethical issues affecting public relations. The second edition follows the format of the first. Chapter 1 has been reorganized from the first edition and a section has been added on applying ethics to the campaign planning process. The remaining chapters examine various aspects of the law that affect public relations. These chapters have been updated to reflect recent case law. The book is not meant to be a comprehensive review of every law affecting the profession. Nor is it meant to take the place of legal advice from an attorney. Its purpose is to increase the familiarity of public relations practitioners with the laws and issues affecting them and to help them ask the right questions.

Notes

[1] Richard A. Mann and Barry S. Roberts, *Contemporary Business Law* (Minneapolis: West, 1996), 2–3.

[2] Kathy Fitzpatrick, "Public Relations and the Law: A Survey of Practitioners," *Public Relations Review* 22 (1996): 1–8.

[3] Morton J. Simon, *Public Relations Law* (New York: Meridith, 1969), 4.

[4] Bryan H. Reber, Fritz Cropp, and Glen T. Cameron, "Mythic Battles: Examining the Lawyer–Public Relations Counselor Dynamic," *Journal of Public Relations Research* 13 (2001): 208.

chapter one

DOING THE RIGHT THING

The practice of public relations is about relationships, and relationships are at the heart of ethics. Ethics is the study of what constitutes right and wrong, or good and bad, human behavior. Communications scholar Mark McElreath has defined ethics as "the set of criteria by which decisions are made about what is right and what is wrong."[1] When applied to public relations, ethics seek to provide a framework to answer such questions as: How far can public relations professionals go in promoting their clients? Are they ever justified in not telling the truth about their clients or in misleading their publics by being selective with the truth?

Thomas Bivins has argued that public relations professionals have moral obligations to:

- themselves (to preserve their own integrity);
- clients (to honor contracts and to use professional expertise on their behalf);
- organizations/employers (to adhere to organizational goals and policies);
- profession/colleagues (to uphold the standards of the profession); and
- society (to consider societal needs and claims).[2]

Public relations professionals need, then, to have a strong sense of business, professional, and personal ethics. Business ethics seek to understand the moral issues that arise from business practices, institutions, and decision making and their relationship to general human values. What is the right ethical decision for a business to make? Drawing management's attention to the potential effects of corporate action on its publics or stakeholders should be one of the public relations professional's roles.

1

At the same time, public relations practitioners are expected to maintain the ethical standards of their profession as set out in the Public Relations Society of America's code of conduct. And finally, but certainly not least, are personal ethics. Public relations professionals may be asked to do things by their employers that they cannot ethically justify on a personal level, such as represent an abortion clinic or a tobacco company. If individuals cannot do their best for their employer or client because of their own personal beliefs, then they should not act for that client. In fact, some have argued that to do so is itself unethical.

The more individuals know about their own ethics and about ethics in general, the better equipped they are to make ethically sound decisions. This chapter will discuss the classical theories of ethics relevant to the practice of public relations, the ethical standards of business, theories of public relations ethics, and codes of ethics. It will also consider personal ethics and the application of ethics to decision making.

Classical Theories

Philosophers have studied ethics for centuries, and as will be seen, there are no easy answers to what constitutes good or right human behavior. For some philosophers, an act is moral if the means used are ethical; for others, an act is moral if its consequences or ends are ethical. Still other philosophers focus on the individual actor rather than the act and consider the actor's intention in acting.

Deontology (Means-Based Ethics)

Deontologists, from the Greek word *deon* (meaning duty or obligation), hold that certain underlying principles are right or wrong, regardless of their consequences. To be moral, a person not only must achieve just results through acts but also must employ the proper means and act with good intentions.

The best-known deontological theory is associated with the eighteenth-century German philosopher Immanuel Kant. Kant argued that moral principles could be known as a result of reason alone. For example, he would say that we do not need to know anything about the consequences of telling a lie to our employer to know it is wrong. For Kant, our actions are moral only when they are done out of our sense of duty to be fair and honest.[3] A moral action must:

- potentially be a universal law that could be applied consistently (what Kant called a categorical imperative); and
- respect the integrity of all humans and not treat them as a means to an end.

To see Kant's reasoning in action, let's look at the example of the Beech-Nut Nutrition Corporation, which was the country's second-largest baby food manufacturer in the early 1980s. Beech-Nut learned in 1982 that a shipment of apple juice concentrate from a supplier was possibly just flavored sugar water. The concentrate was used to make the company's apple juice for babies that it sold as 100 percent pure. At the time, it was difficult for chemists to detect beet sugar or other sugars in apple juice, but in case the shipment really was not apple juice, the company decided to return the unused concentrate and not purchase any further product from the supplier. That decision was an easy one. The more difficult question was what to do with its inventory of cases of finished product containing the questionable concentrate.[4] If we apply the Kantian form of reasoning, the company would take its inventory off the market until it was able to ascertain whether the concentrate was from apples or had been adulterated. Such an action would be moral in Kant's terms because it can be applied consistently (no company should continue to market potentially misleading products) and it respects the integrity of Beech-Nut's consumers..Kant's philosophy rejects the notion that the end justifies the means. To Kant, every person is an end in him- or herself. Each person deserves respect simply because of his or her humanity.

Today, deontological thinking can be seen in codes of ethics and standards of conduct, which provide proscriptions for behavior. Having clear rules about what constitutes ethical behavior can be very comforting, and that is the advantage of deontology. At the same, however, the philosophy is criticized often precisely for that certainty. Rigid guidelines are helpful, but they may not apply to every situation. For example, to adopt telling the truth as an absolute rule leads one to ignore situations in which lying may well be justified. A person hiding an abused wife would seem to be acting morally in lying about her whereabouts to her husband. But a deontologist would feel a duty to tell the truth regardless of the potential danger to the wife.[5]

Another criticism of deontology is that one culture may consider an action universally moral, but another culture might not find it so.[6] And often decisions in business are not matters of choosing to honor a duty or obligation or not, but of choosing between two rights or two obligations. W. D. Ross attempted to overcome that criticism by arguing that what one ought to do will depend on the circumstances and the relative importance of the conflicting obligations.[7] What must be decided is which of the obligations is more important in the given circumstances. In the example of the wife hiding from her abusive husband, while Kant would have said that telling the truth is a categorical imperative, Ross would have said that the obligation to tell the truth can be outweighed by other moral factors. Ross recognized that there may be conflicting obligations—obligations to employees, shareholders, and consumers—that may pull an organization in different directions.

In these situations, determining the corporation's proper moral course may not be easy. Beech-Nut, for example, obviously had an obligation to its consumers, but it also had obligations to its employees, its corporate owner, Nestle, S.A., and in turn to Nestle's shareholders. The company had suffered significant financial losses in the 1970s but was just beginning to see positive growth from efforts to improve its products and image when the apple juice incident occurred. The publicity of the concentrate problem and the cost of destroying the product could well have been financially disastrous for the company.[8]

To deal with the difficulty of deciding between competing obligations, Ross proposed a set of prima facie duties that should be honored:

- Duty of fidelity
- Duty of gratitude
- Duty of justice
- Duty of beneficence
- Duty of self-improvement
- Duty of noninjury

Ross said to choose the most important duty when there was conflict, but he provided no guidelines for making that decision. Thus, Ross provides no help in determining Beech-Nut's best course of action.

Consequentialism (Ends-Based Ethics)

Many philosophers have argued that the moral rightness of an action is determined solely by its results. Actions themselves are neither moral nor immoral. An action is good if its consequences are good; an action is bad if its consequences are bad. One question that arises, of course, is consequences for whom? An example of the consequentialist philosophy is utilitarianism. Utilitarians take the position that the ethical act is the one that produces the greatest possible balance of good over bad for everyone affected. In the eighteenth century, Jeremy Bentham, one of the most influential proponents of utilitarianism, said that a good or moral act is one that results in the "greatest good for the greatest number."[9] Determining the "greatest good" and the "greatest number," however, can be problematic. In the Beech-Nut example, would destroying all of the apple juice inventory and potentially forcing the company into bankruptcy be the greatest good for the greatest number when there was no suggestion that the product was dangerous or that consumers would even notice it was not 100 percent apple juice? Or would leaving the inventory on the market and remaining financially viable for its shareholders and employees result in the greatest good for the greatest number?

Critics of the utilitarian approach are concerned with its potential unpredictability. They also point out that it sometimes simply ignores justice. For example, utilitarianism would condone harming a few individuals if the rest of society would ultimately benefit. Beech-Nut's ultimate decision to continue to sell the product despite knowing it was not 100 percent apple juice, while ethical under utilitarian standards, sacrifices consumers for the company's long-term economic viability. Many philosophers are also critical of utilitarianism because it reduces all morality to a concern with consequences and views humans as means rather than as ends in themselves.

Distributive Justice

Because of the potential for the majority to always win out to the detriment of the minority under utilitarian reasoning, the theory of distributive justice is used to protect minority rights. In 1971, the American philosopher John Rawls argued that if individuals were put under a "veil of ignorance" such that they did not know their social position or their abilities in society, they would agree to be governed by certain principles of justice.[10] Essentially, he argued that individuals unfamiliar with social rules and expectations would advocate a system of distributive justice based on fairness. Rawls stated two principles of justice: (a) each individual has an equal claim to basic rights and liberties and (b) any social and economic inequality among individuals is permitted, but only if there has been equality of opportunity. For Rawls, then, a moral society is one that considers the needs and rights of all its members.

If Beech-Nut had balanced its decision based on utilitarianism with distributive justice, the company would have advised consumers that the product may not be 100 percent pure and allowed consumers to make their own decision about whether to purchase it.

Egoism

Beech-Nut's decision to protect its reputation and minimize economic losses is an example of egoist ethics. Egoism, or enlightened self-interest, contends that an act is morally right if, and only if, it best promotes the individual's long-term interests. If an action produces, or will probably produce, more good than evil for the individual in the long run than any other alternative, then the action is the right one to take.

Critics of egoism argue that self-interest can never be the basis of ethical decision making, because ethics involves consideration of other humans. David Martinson has argued that ethical behavior requires genuine sacrifice and that doing what is in one's own interest does not amount to sacrifice.[11] According to Martinson, a company should, for example, issue a recall because it is the morally right thing to do, not because it will increase profits in the long term.

To counter such criticism, defenders of egoism say that egoism is different from ordinary self-interest because of its focus on the long term. In fact, in the short term, an action may be against the company's self-interest, either because the action will increase the cost of the product, or because the company will have to publicly admit it made a mistake. Patricia Whalen has suggested that enlightened self-interest has within its definition an expressed desire to bring benefit to society because the organization is a member of that society.[12] The concept is based on the premise that a healthy corporation cannot exist in an unhealthy community. Self-interest, on the other hand, is more limited. It views the corporation as a separate entity that operates in its own self-interest with no consideration of the effects of its actions on others.

Virtue Ethics (Actor-Based Ethics)

While some philosophers debate whether the means or the ends determine ethical behavior, others look to the individual actor rather than the act. The focus is on what makes an individual ethical instead of on what is the right thing to do. Aristotle, for instance, was interested in what makes a person good. What virtues do they have? Aristotle reasoned that individuals who learned good habits of character would naturally do what was right. And what was right was a mean between the two extremes of excess and deficiency. Thus, his theory is known as the golden mean. He saw moderation as the path to a virtuous life. For example, courage is the mean between fear and confidence. Too much fear and too little confidence can lead to cowardice. Too little fear and too much confidence can lead to foolhardy acts. But the mean was not to be determined by a mathematical formula. It was to be determined through moral reasoning and the individual's circumstances. The individual who was morally mature would naturally determine the right thing to do.[13]

To the extent that public relations seeks to create mutually beneficial relationships between the organization and its publics, public relations can be seen as helping organizations seek Aristotle's golden mean. For example, according to widely endorsed standards of corporate conduct, one corporate virtue is transparency. Transparency is the mean between being closed to outside scrutiny and disclosing everything. The appropriate level of transparency will depend on legal constraints, but it will consist of being open about decisions that affect others such that they understand why a particular decision was made.

The importance of Aristotle's golden mean and virtue ethics to public relations is that they remind us that character does make a difference. A virtuous person will do the right thing more often than not. A person who does not have a strong sense of his or her own values will not. A criticism of Aristotle's theory, however, is that it does not provide a process for decision making; it just assumes that a person of good character will do what is right.

Ethical Standards in Business

Any discussion of business ethics must begin with the question of whether a corporation, which is an artificial entity created by the state, has ethical responsibilities. The same question can be asked about any organization, not just businesses. Clearly, the individuals within an organization or corporation can be held morally responsible for their actions. But can an organization itself be held responsible for its actions? Some ethicists argue that only people can engage in moral or immoral behavior. Others agree that corporations are not persons literally but insist that corporate behavior can and should be judged from a moral perspective. One thing is clear: Acting ethically is often advantageous for companies. Research has shown that ethical practices are actually beneficial to the bottom line.[14]

Profit Maximization

Economist Milton Friedman, writing in the 1960s, argued that the sole obligation of business was to maximize profit while engaging in open and free competition without deception or fraud.[15] Thus, for Friedman, so long as a business conducted itself within the boundaries of the law, it was fulfilling its societal responsibilities. Its primary obligation was to its owners or shareholders.

Social Responsibility

Friedman's laissez-faire attitude toward business and society fell out of favor in the 1970s. Corporate and government scandals and the rise of the consumer movement in the early 1970s led to a push for greater social responsibility on the part of corporations.[16] This movement gave rise to a new organizational model, the self-moralizing corporation, which stressed individual moral behavior within the organization and the development of a moral culture.[17] The argument of those adopting the self-moralizing model is that moral responsibility is the self-imposed duty to ensure that one's actions do not intentionally or knowingly cause harm to others. Corporations are not rational beings, but they are established by, and their actions are determined by, rational beings. Therefore, officers of corporations must ultimately assume responsibility for the corporations' actions.

Criticism of Social Responsibility

Although Friedman's profit maximization theory has lost favor, remnants of his thinking remain among critics of corporate social responsibility. Simcha Werner, for example, has questioned how far a corporation has to go in protecting society.[18] Is the company required to go to the verge of bankruptcy to clean up the environment, or is it enough to meet the legal regulations for environmental protection?

Jerry Mander has argued that the idea of a corporate conscience is just a myth.[19] A corporation is not just the sum of the people who work for it, but rather a separate legal entity that is amoral. Corporations, he argued, must operate within certain laws and rules regardless of the people inside it, and to view corporations as an aggregation of people is to exhibit business naiveté. A corporate manager cannot place community welfare above the corporation's interests because to do so would open management up to lawsuits from shareholders. As others have argued, spending corporate profits to benefit society is unethical in itself because those profits belong to the shareholders, not to the corporation or its managers.

Theories of Public Relations Ethics

An understanding of business ethics is important for public relations practitioners, but just as important is an understanding of how ethical frameworks have been applied in a public relations context. Public relations as corporate conscience fits well with the business ethic of social responsibility. And as interest in business ethics has grown, so too has research into the ethical practices of public relations professionals, which shows that the predominant ethical framework used by public relations professionals is situational ethics; that is, public relations professionals respond differently to the same ethical situations according to their own personal values.[20] They have a tendency to make ends-based choices that shift from situation to situation.

In response, a number of theories or ethical approaches have been developed to guide the practice of public relations. Some scholars, such as Richard Nelson, argue that a framework anchored in deontology—one based on duty—would provide greater consistency.[21] An action would be right or wrong, regardless of its consequences, under such an approach. Others argue that deontological approaches are not practical in the workplace and that a utilitarian approach would provide more guidance.[22]

Three approaches to ethical public relations will be discussed here: communitarianism, dialogic/discourse ethics, and value ethics. Also discussed will be criteria for ethical advocacy or persuasion.

Communitarianism

Communitarianism stresses the community and the ties that bind individuals together. It calls for a movement away from the emphasis on individual rights to that of social responsibility. When applied to public relations, communitarianism means that public relations professionals should encourage organizations to recognize and fulfill their responsibilities to the communities of which they are a part. As Kathie Leeper noted, "A communitarian approach would suggest that what is best for the community is ultimately in the best interests of the organization."[23] In the Beech-Nut example, although the product was not dangerous, a communitarian approach would have required the company to pull all of the product or at least disclose the scientific results.

Dialogic/Discourse Ethics

Dialogic communication and discourse ethics share an emphasis on dialogue. Dialogic communication is most often associated with the philosophy of Martin Buber.[24] Buber viewed communication as a process that occurs when individuals treat each other with openness and respect. The product of such a relationship is dialogue. As Michael Kent and Maureen Taylor have noted, for a dialogic relationship to exist, communication must be seen as an end in itself.[25]

This view of communication has also been the cornerstone of Jürgen Habermas's theory of discourse ethics.[26] Inherent in Habermas's theory is the notion that ethical communication or dialogue cannot be dominated by any one party. Dialogue, by definition, suggests a cooperative, give-and-take form of communication based on mutual respect and compromise. To that end, Habermas set out four criteria necessary for ethical communication:

1. It must be comprehensible.

2. It must be true.

3. It must be appropriate for the audience.

4. It must be sincere.

In addition to these four requirements, Ronald Pearson set out four conditions necessary for ethical public relations based on Habermas's theory:[27]

5. There must be the opportunity for beginning and ending communicative interaction.

6. There must be the opportunity for suggesting topics and initiating topic changes.

7. There must be the ability to provide a response and to have that response treated as such.

8. There must be the ability to select channels of communication.

Combined, the eight criteria listed above form a framework for ethical public relations. Under the dialogic approach, Beech-Nut should have communicated openly and honestly with consumers about the true nature of its apple juice and provided a means to receive their feedback. Such an approach would have allowed consumers to make informed decisions about the product.

Value Ethics

Writing in the 1960s, Albert Sullivan identified two value systems operating in public relations in which ethical considerations come into play:

- partisan, which includes the values of loyalty, commitment, and obedience to an employer or organization, and

- mutuality, which takes into account the interests and rights of others.[28]

It is the value system of mutuality that leads to truly ethical public relations for Sullivan because it requires companies to consider the following basic rights of individuals:

- the right to accurate and complete information regarding matters that affect them;

- the right to participate in decisions that affect them; and

- the right to have their rights respected by others.

Sullivan's concepts, like the dialogic approach, require public relations professionals to ensure that their organizations provide publics with accurate information and an opportunity for participation.

Ethical Advocacy

Drawing on many of the above ethical frameworks, Ruth Edgett has devised a set of criteria for practicing ethical advocacy or persuasion.[29] A criticism of some of the ethical approaches developed for public relations practice is that they ignore persuasion as a function of public relations. Persuasion is treated as though it is unethical by its nature. But persuasive communication, or rhetoric, has a long history, beginning with the study of rhetoric by the ancient Greeks. And as Edgett has argued, persuasion can be practiced ethically, provided certain criteria are followed:

- **Evaluation.** Practitioners first should objectively evaluate the situation and the client to determine whether persuasion is warranted.

- **Priority.** In advocating for clients, practitioners must put their clients' interests first.

- **Sensitivity.** At the same time, however, practitioners must balance their clients' interests against their social responsibility.

- **Confidentiality.** Practitioners must respect and protect their clients' confidentiality on all matters ethically and legally requiring confidentiality.

- **Veracity.** In the process of persuading others, practitioners must practice full truthfulness.

- **Reversibility.** In determining veracity, practitioners should put themselves in the place of the target audience and consider whether sufficient information has been given for the audience to make an informed decision.

- **Validity.** Practitioners must ensure that the persuasive communication can withstand attacks on its validity.

- **Visibility.** Practitioners must ensure that the communication clearly identifies the clients.

- **Respect.** Practitioners must ensure that they treat all audiences as autonomous, with the right to make informed decisions.

- **Consent.** Persuasive communication must only occur in situations where it can be assumed that all parties consent.

Codes of Ethics

One of the signs of professionalism is a code of ethics governing the conduct of members of the profession. Codes of ethics serve two purposes: (1) they are a continual reminder to members of the profession of the acceptable standards of behavior for that profession and (2) they assure those outside of the profession that ethical standards are maintained within the profession's ranks.[30]

PRSA Member Code of Ethics

The Public Relations Society of America (PRSA), founded in 1948, adopted its Code of Professional Standards for the Practice of Public Relations in 1950. It did so to meet three goals:

- to provide behavioral guidelines to its members;
- to educate management on public relations standards; and
- to distinguish public relations professionals from those individuals who use the title but are perceived as giving the profession a bad name.[31]

In 2000, PRSA adopted a new code of ethics for its members. This code differs from earlier PRSA codes of ethics in three important ways. First, it eliminated the emphasis on enforcement, although the PRSA retained the right to bar membership to an individual or expel a member for ethical breaches. Second, the new code focuses on universal values inspiring ethical behavior. Third, the code illustrates appropriate behavior through guidelines and examples for easy use.

The 2000 code begins with a statement of six professional values that PRSA believes are "vital to the integrity of the professional as a whole."[32]

- **Advocacy.** Public relations professionals serve the public interest by acting as responsible advocates for clients and provide a voice in the marketplace of ideas to aid informed public debate.
- **Honesty.** Public relations professionals adhere to the highest standards of accuracy and truth.
- **Expertise.** Public relations professionals have specialized knowledge and skill and maintain that knowledge and skill through continued professional development.

- **Independence**. Public relations professionals provide objective advice to their clients and are accountable for their actions.
- **Loyalty**. Public relations professionals are loyal to their clients but continue to serve the public interest.
- **Fairness**. Public relations professionals treat fairly all publics, including clients.

The code goes on to set out core principles governing the ethical practice of public relations. These principles include:

- protecting and advancing the free flow of information;
- promoting healthy and fair competition among professionals;
- promoting open and honest disclosure of information;
- safeguarding confidential and private information of clients;
- avoiding real, potential, or perceived conflicts of interest; and
- enhancing the public's trust in the profession.

At the heart of these principles is an acknowledgement of the fundamental value and dignity of the individual and the importance of freedom of expression to the practice of public relations. To adhere to these ethical principles, Beech-Nut's public relations counselors should have advised the company to be fair and honest in its dealings with the public.

Global Business Standards Codex

The business sector is too varied to have a code of ethics, although each business may choose to develop their own. In fact, the Global Business Standards Codex is a compilation of standards commonly found in individual company codes of conduct. The codex sets out eight basic principles that are similar to the principles in the PRSA code of ethics. The principles include:

- acting in the best interests of the company and its investors;
- respecting property and the rights of those who own it;
- keeping promises, agreements, contracts, and other commitments;
- conducting business in a truthful and open manner;
- respecting the dignity of all people;
- dealing fairly with all parties;
- acting as responsible members of the community; and

- being responsive to the legitimate claims and concerns of others.[33]

Clearly Beech-Nut violated several of these principles when it chose to sell its inventory as 100 percent pure when it had doubts about the veracity of that claim.

International Codes of Conduct

Today, ethics in public relations and business encompass a worldwide stage. The International Public Relations Association (IPRA) and the International Association of Business Communicators (IABC) are two groups that not only promote matters of ethical practices, but also cultural sensitivity. In its Code of Ethics for Professional Communicators, the IABC has stated that professional communication should be legal, ethical, and in good taste. "These principles assume that just societies are governed by a profound respect for human rights and the rule of law; that ethics, the criteria for determining what is right and wrong, can be agreed upon by members of an organization; and, that understanding matters of taste requires sensitivity to cultural norms."[34]

Criticism of Ethical Codes

Codes of conduct are not without their detractors. One criticism is that codes are too general to be of much help in a real situation. The 2000 PRSA code of ethics attempts to address that criticism by providing guidelines and examples of what is and is not ethical behavior. The idea is to make the code practical for use in day-to-day situations. Another criticism is that there can be contradictions within the codes themselves. For example, in the PRSA code, public relations professionals are required to safeguard confidences of their client, while at the same time being open and honest with the public. There may be times when honoring both of these obligations puts the public relations professional into a position of conflict.

A third criticism is the lack of enforcement. Public relations practitioners are not licensed as lawyers and doctors are; therefore, if the PRSA were to find a practitioner guilty of unethical conduct, the most serious penalty it can impose is suspension of membership in the association. Membership in the PRSA is not a requirement for practicing public relations. In fact, many public relations professionals are not members. Because the PRSA has removed the enforcement emphasis from its code and now relies on education to encourage compliance, no external motivation exists for obeying the code. The PRSA must rely solely on the individual ethics of its members.

Universal Code of Ethics

Some scholars criticize codes of ethics for claiming to be universal when they are not. They assume that everyone, regardless of situation and culture, abides by the same ethical standards. Despite this criticism, there is a push in public relations to create a universal code of ethics. Todd Hunt and Andrew Tirpok have argued that such a code is possible if based on the ideals of social responsibility. Dean Kruckeberg also has argued that a universal code is possible and feasible because a universal basis of morality can be found. But, as other scholars point out, when public relations practices around the world are discussed, U.S. customs are seen by Americans as the "norm" and practices in other countries are seen as "other." The result is an attempt to impose American standards on other countries, something known as cultural imperialism.[35] A universal public relations code of ethics, according to these scholars, would really be just an American public relations code of ethics imposed on the rest of the world.

Personal Ethics

Lewis and Reinscht have argued that an individual's professional ethics cannot be separated from that individual's personal ethics. Public relations research shows that public relations professionals apply their personal ethics in professional situations.[36]

Research by psychologist Lawrence Kohlberg suggests that moral growth is part of the human condition. Kohlberg observed that people progress through stages of moral development according to two major variables—age and education. He described three major levels:

- **Preconventional.** At the preconventional level, children behave well because they fear punishment or seek a reward. Although people who operate at this level may behave morally, they do so without understanding why their behavior is moral. The rules are imposed on them from the outside.

- **Conventional.** During adolescence, most people begin to conform to the expectations of groups, such as family, peers, and society. Loyalty, affection, and trust motivate conformity. Most adults remain at this level.

- **Postconventional.** According to Kohlberg, only a few adults reach the postconventional level. At this stage, individuals accept and conform to moral principles because they understand why the principles are right and binding. At this level, moral principles are voluntarily internalized, not externally imposed. Moreover, individuals at this stage develop their own universal ethical principles and may even question the laws and values that society and others have adopted.[37]

Other psychologists believe that individuals do not pass from stage to stage but function in all stages simultaneously.

Application

The ethical practice of public relations involves consideration of the interests of various stakeholders and publics. But it can be difficult to balance the interests of all of these publics with the interests of the organization itself. The ethical challenge is to find a model that "describes the threshold beyond which advancement of the client's interests becomes overly destructive to society's interest."[38] Ideally, ethics should be incorporated into every aspect of public relations, including the campaign planning process, to help head off ethical dilemmas. A combination of classical theories and tests can be used at each step.

At the beginning of the planning process, you want to know that you are acting for the right reasons in developing the campaign. You want to seek Aristotle's golden mean in the sense that you want to be the virtuous practitioner. You do not want to be overly gullible about your organization's or client's motives for the campaign; nor do you want to be overly skeptical about them. You want to bring your independence and expertise to bear and provide appropriate counsel to the organization.[39] Thus, you should ensure your intent is ethical while conducting research and setting objectives.

As you develop your strategies, you could conduct an SOCS (stakeholders, options, consequences, and strategy) analysis to determine the consequences of each strategy on your publics. To do so, you first identify all of the stakeholders who will be affected by your campaign. Then, you set out the various options or strategies you have and the consequences of each for every stakeholders. You would then select the strategy that does the greatest good for the greatest number.[40]

When developing your tactics, you want to ensure that they do not violate any legal regulations and that they satisfy your professional (PRSA, IABC) code of conduct and the TARES test.

The TARES test was developed by Sherry Baker and David Martinson to evaluate public relations communications and consists of the following:

- **Truthfulness of the message.** Does the communication provide the audience with sufficient information to make an informed decision on the issue?

- **Authenticity of the persuader.** What is the motive of the communicator? Will someone other than the communicator benefit from the message?

- **Respect for the persuadee.** Does the message treat the public with respect and as human beings?

- **Equity of the appeal.** Does the communication take advantage of a public's vulnerabilities?

- **Social responsibility for the common good.** Does the message serve the larger public good?[41]

Applying the TARES test to campaign messages will allow you to assess the ethics of those messages using a deontological (means-based) approach. Edgett's framework for ethical advocacy could also be applied to the messages.

In considering how you will evaluate the campaign, you should consider the consequences of the campaign. Will it do the greatest good for the greatest number? To answer that question, you can conduct a benefit/harm analysis or return to your SOCS analysis.

While deliberate attention to ethics in the planning process will help you avoid ethical dilemmas during a campaign, problems may arise in your day-to-day work environment that you had not anticipated, for ethical dilemmas are not usually black or white. For instance, a public relations practitioner may be asked to write a news release announcing the launch of a client's new product but is told not to mention an internal engineering report that suggests the product needs more testing before being sold to the public. PRSA has developed an ethical decision guide to help practitioners work through such problems:

- **Define the problem**. The first step when faced with an ethical dilemma is to figure out exactly what the ethical conflict is.
- **Identify factors**. Then, you identify the factors that may influence your decision.
- **Identify key values at stake**. As discussed previously, the PRSA code sets out six principle values: advocacy, honesty, expertise, independence, loyalty, and fairness.
- **Identify parties affected**. Identify the parties potentially affected by your decision and your obligation to each.
- **Select ethical principles**. Choose one of the approaches (means based, ends based, actor based) to guide your decision.
- **Make decision and justify it**.

The goal in ethical dilemmas is to choose the resolution that most resembles the right thing to do in the circumstances. If nothing else, you want to think about the consequences of your decision. One way to approach these situations is to ask yourself, "Would I want people reading about what I've done in the newspaper tomorrow morning?" If the answer is no, you may want to rethink your decision.

But what if making the ethically correct decision means going against your boss? It is easy to do in theory, not so easy in practice. The first step is to tell your boss your decision and then justify it. In the situation with the news release, explaining to your boss the risk of lawsuits the company faces and the negative publicity should anything happen to a consumer using the product may well cause him to change his mind. If your boss still insists on going forward as planned, then you have three choices. You can ask to be removed from the account, you can prepare the release as requested, or you can resign. Sometimes the first option is not available because there is no one else who can take over. In that case, you have to decide whether you can live with the consequences of going against your own better judgment. If you cannot, if you feel too strongly about the issue, then you will have to resign. Again, it is an easy decision to make in theory, but a difficult one in practice when you have a mortgage, a car payment, day care, and people financially dependent on you. Usually it will not come to so extreme a point, but at some time in your career you may have to put your personal and professional integrity above your job. One individual who worked for Beech-Nut chose to do just that. He quit when he could not get upper management to take his concerns about the supplier of the apple juice concentrate seriously.

Beech-Nut's failure to act ethically and to continue selling an adulterated product as 100 percent pure put "careers, profits, reputations and public trust in the company at risk."[42] In 1987, the company pleaded guilty to 215 felony counts of shipping adulterated and misbranded juice with intent to mislead and defraud consumers. It was fined $2 million, which was at the time more than six times the largest fine ever paid under the Food, Drug and Cosmetic Act. In addition, the company agreed to pay $7.5 million to settle a class-action lawsuit brought by a supermarket chain. The president of the company was fined $100,000 and sentenced to five years probation and six months community service work. As the *Boston Globe* stated in 1989, "As the publicity about the scandal has waned, Beech-Nut's sales have improved, but only slightly. It cannot shed the stigma of trying to fool the public—especially the public's children."[43]

Summary

Ethics is the study of right and wrong behavior. Philosophers have considered ethics in terms of the intent of the actor, the means used by the actor, and the ends or consequences of the action. Public relations practitioners ought to consciously evaluate each step in the campaign process against ethical standards to ensure ethical behavior. A SOCS analysis and the TARES test can be effective in that evaluation. But, when faced with an ethical dilemma, practitioners should determine the values in competition and the obligation they owe to the various publics affected and then decide which ethical approach would be the best in the circumstances.

Discussion Questions

1. Relate communitarianism, dialogic/discourse ethics, and value ethics to the values and principles set out in the PRSA's code of conduct. What features do they have in common? What does that tell you about the ethical practice of public relations?

2. In many countries, it is common practice to pay a media outlet for running a news release. Although considered unethical by American standards, can such a practice be ethical? In other words, are ethics universal, or are they culturally based? Can there ever be a universal code of ethics for public relations practice?

3. Fresh out of university, you decide to open your own public relations firm in your hometown. Your first client is a local microbrewery. The brewery has been successful to date because it turns out a good product and has little competition in the area. The owner thinks it is now time to expand and comes to you for help in promoting the brewery. You propose a tour of the facility for the media and community leaders.

   Your tour idea is a great success with 60 people, including members of the media, expected to arrive. An hour before the tour begins, the owner tells you that a test has shown there may be bacteria in the batch of beer that is to be served to the guests. The test is not conclusive, and the bacteria, even if present, does not pose a real health risk. You know that everyone is expecting free beer on the tour. You also know that the media would love to get their hands on a story about bacteria in the beer. Several influential people in town have made attempts in the past to close down the brewery. Dangerous beer would add fuel to the fire. You consider serving the beer anyway, hoping that the test is in error. But your best friend, a reporter, is coming to the tour, and she is extremely susceptible to any kind of bacteria. Consider the ethical ramifications of your actions for the microbrewery.

Notes

[1] Mark P. McElreath, *Managing Systematic and Ethical Public Relations* (Dubuque, IA: Brown & Benchmark, 1993), 320.

[2] Thomas H. Bivins, "A Systems Model for Ethical Decision Making in Public Relations," *Public Relations Review* 18 (1992): 365–383.

[3] Cornelius B. Pratt, "Critique of the Classical Theory of Situational Ethics in U.S. Public Relations," *Public Relations Review* 19 (1993): 219–234.

[4] Morton Mintz, "Careers, Trust at Stake in Beech-Nut Trial," *Washington Post*, November 29, 1987, p. H2; James Traub, "Into the Mouths of Babes," *New York Times*, July 24, 1988, S.6, p. 18.

[5] Richard A. Mann and Barry S. Roberts, *Contemporary Business Law* (Minneapolis: West, 1996).

6 Ibid.

7 W. D. Ross, *The Right and the Good* (London: Oxford University Press, 1930).

8 Traub, "Into the Mouths of Babes."

9 Quoted in William H. Shaw and Vincent Barry, *Moral Issues in Business*, 6th ed. (Belmont, CA: Wadsworth, 1995), 61.

10 John Rawls, *A Theory of Justice* (Cambridge, MA: Belknap, 1971).

11 David L. Martinson, "Enlightened Self-interest Fails as an Ethical Baseline in Public Relations," *Journal of Mass Media Ethics* 9 (1994): 100–108.

12 Patricia T. Whalen, "Enlightened Self-interest—An Ethical Baseline for Teaching Corporate Public Relations," paper presented at the meeting of the American Educators in Journalism and Mass Communication, Baltimore, MD, August 1998.

13 Richard Kraut, "Aristotle's Ethics," *The Stanford Encyclopedia of Philosophy* (June 3, 2005), ed. Edward N. Zalta, http://plato.stanford.edu/entries/aristotle-ethics/ (accessed April 5, 2007).

14 Simcha B. Werner, "The Movement for Reforming American Business Ethics: A Twenty-year Perspective," *Journal of Business Ethics* 11 (1992): 61–70; Kathie A. Leeper, "Public Relations Ethics and Communitarianism: A Preliminary Investigation," *Public Relations Review* 22 (1996): 163–179.

15 Milton Friedman, *Capitalism and Freedom* (Chicago: University of Chicago Press, 1963).

16 Werner, "The Movement for Reforming."

17 Ibid.

18 Ibid.

19 Jerry Mander, "The Myth of the Corporate Conscience," *Business and Society Review* 80 (1992): 56–63.

20 Donald K. Wright, "Examining Ethical and Moral Values of Public Relations People," *Public Relations Review* 15 (1989): 19–33.

21 Richard A. Nelson, "Issues Communication and Advocacy: Contemporary Ethical Challenges," *Public Relations Review* 20 (1994): 225–231.

22 See Bivins, "A Systems Model."

23 Leeper, "Public Relations Ethics," 173.

24 Michael L. Kent and Maureen Taylor, "Building Dialogic Relationships through the World Wide Web," *Public Relations Review* 24 (1998): 321–334.

25 Ibid.

26 Roy V. Leeper, "Moral Objectivity, Jürgen Habermas' Discourse Ethics, and Public Relations," *Public Relations Review* 22 (1996): 133–150.

27 Ronald Pearson, "Beyond Ethical Relativism in Public Relations: Coorientation, Rules, and the Idea of Communication Symmetry," in J. E. Grunig and L. A. Grunig, eds., *Public Relations Research Annual*, vol. 1: 6786 (Hillsdale, NJ: Erlbaum).

28 Albert J. Sullivan, "Values in Public Relations," in O. Lerbinger and A. Sullivan, eds., *Information, Influence, and Communication: A Reader in Public Relations* (New York: Basic Books, 1965), 412–439; see also Ronald Pearson, "Albert J. Sullivan's Theory of Public Relations Ethics," *Public Relations Review* 15 (1989): 52–62.

29 Ruth Edgett, "Toward an Ethical Framework for Advocacy in Public Relations," *Journal of Public Relations Research* 14 (2002): 1–26.

30 Cornelius Pratt, "Critique of the Classical Theory of Situational Ethics in U.S. Public Relations," *Public Relations Review* 19 (1993): 219–234.

31 Kathie A. Leeper, "Public Relations Ethics and Communitarianism: A Preliminary Investigation," *Public Relations Review* 22 (1996): 163–179.

[32] Public Relations Society of America, "Preamble," *Member Code of Ethics 2000*, http://www.prsa.org/aboutUs/ethics/preamble_en.html (accessed May 14, 2007).

[33] Lynn S. Paine, Rohit Deshpandé, Joshua D. Margolis, and Kim E. Bettcher, "Up to Code: Does Your Company's Conduct Meet World-Class Standards?" *Harvard Business Review* 83(12) (December 2005): 122–133.

[34] International Association of Business Communicators, "Code of Ethics for Professional Communicators," http://www.iabc.com/about/code.htm (accessed May 14, 2007).

[35] Todd Hunt and Andrew Tirpok, "Universal Ethics Code: An Idea Whose Time Has Come," *Public Relations Review* 19 (1993): 1–11; Dean Kruckeberg, "Universal Ethics Code: Both Possible and Feasible," *Public Relations Review* 19 (1993): 21–31; Nancy Roth, Todd Hunt, Maria Stavropoulos, and Karen Black, "Can't We All Just Get Along?: Cultural Variables in Codes of Ethics," *Public Relations Review* 22 (1996): 151–161.

[36] P. V. Lewis and N. L. Reinscht, "Ethical and Unethical Behaviors in Business Communication," in *Business Communication: The Corporate Connection*, ed. S. J. Bruno, Proceedings of the 1983 American Business Communication Convention, 1983, 3–13; see also Jacob Shamir, Barbara Strauss Reed, and Steven Connell, "Individual Differences in Ethical Values of Public Relations Practitioners," *Journalism Quarterly* 67 (1990): 956–963; Donald Wright, "Individual Ethics Determine Public Relations Practice," *Public Relations Journal* (April 1985): 38–39.

[37] Lawrence Kohlberg, *Essays on Moral Development: Vol. 1. The Philosophy of Moral Development* (New York: Harper & Row, 1981).

[38] Ralph D. Barney and Jay Black, "Ethics and Professional Persuasive Communications," *Public Relations Review* 20 (1994): 233–248.

[39] Elspeth Tilley, "The Ethics Pyramid: Making Ethics Unavoidable in the Public Relations Process," *Journal of Mass Media Ethics* 20(4) (2005): 305–320.

[40] Ibid.

[41] Sherry Baker and David L. Martinson, "The TARES Test: Five Principles for Ethical Persuasion," *Journal of Mass Media Ethics* 16 (2001): 148–175.

[42] Mintz, "Careers, Trust at Stake."

[43] Editorial, "Beech-Nut's Unforgivable Sin," *Boston Globe*, July 10, 1989, p. 16.

chapter two

DEFINING
PUBLIC RELATIONS SPEECH

The essence of public relations is managing relationships through communication. This combination of management and communication means that public relations professionals need an understanding of not only laws affecting communication, but also of those affecting business. As with all communicators, the speech of public relations professionals can be subject to lawsuits for defamation and invasions of privacy. Another risk is that public relations professionals may infringe the copyright and trademark rights of others.

Public relations speech differs from other communication, however, in that it gives a voice to corporations and often has a commercial purpose. As a result, the speech aspect of public relations is subsumed under two different First Amendment categories of speech: corporate and commercial. Corporate speech is speech by corporations concerning political and social issues. Commercial speech, on the other hand, is speech more directly related to the promotion of a product or service.

This chapter will provide an overview of the sources of law. It will then look at the First Amendment, which protects speech from governmental regulation, and the philosophical justifications for protecting freedom of expression. Finally, it will discuss corporate and commercial speech.

Sources of Law

The United States has four primary sources of law: constitutional, statutory, common, and administrative. The U.S. Constitution is the highest law in the land; it sets out the parameters under which each branch of the federal government operates. It also provides the limits for governmental actions against individuals. State constitutions provide the second-highest law. State constitutions can provide greater individual protections from governmental interference, but not less protection than the U.S. Constitution.

The second source of law is statutory. Congress and state legislatures pass statutes that govern behavior. State statutes often codify the common law. Common law, the third source, is judge-made law built on precedent. It legalizes the common custom of the state. The common law evolves constantly, along with society, but the process of change is slow and uneven. When a quick response is needed to address a situation, such as the corporate accounting scandals involving Enron and WorldCom in 2002, statutory law is the most effective.

The final source of law, administrative, governs the conduct and duties of government agencies. These agencies, such as the Securities and Exchange Commission, make rules, enforce them, and adjudicate disputes about the rules.

All four sources of law affect to some degree how and what public relations practitioners communicate, but as the highest law in the land, the U.S. Constitution's coverage of public relations speech sets the tone for the rest of the law.

Development of First Amendment Law

The First Amendment is the first of the ten amendments to the U.S. Constitution that form what is known as the Bill of Rights. It states that "Congress shall make no law respecting an establishment of religion, or prohibiting the free exercise thereof; or abridging the freedom of speech, or of the press; or the right of the people peaceably to assemble, and to petition the Government for a redress of grievances." The provision essentially provides that the government cannot restrict an individual's right to speak regardless of what the government might think about the speech. The First Amendment originally referred only to government at the federal level, but today it applies to state governments as well.

Despite its absolute language, the First Amendment has never been interpreted to mean that all speech is protected. In fact, it is unclear what the exact meaning of the provision was to its framers. Scholars agree that it meant at least freedom from prior restraint or licensing. Sir William Blackstone, a British legal scholar, in 1765 defined freedom of expression as "laying no previous restraint upon publications."[1] In other words, there could be no licensing, monopolies, or anything that required the government's approval before printing. Some scholars, however, argue that the First Amendment supplies more than simply freedom from prior restraint.[2] They argue that it also supplies freedom from punishment for such offenses as criticizing the government.

Over the years, the First Amendment has come to mean whatever the U.S. Supreme Court says it means at any particular time. Its meaning and the resulting level of freedom of expression tolerated by Americans vary—changes can result from historical context. For instance, after the terrorist attacks of September 11, 2001, freedom to express one's opinion, especially if that opinion was against the Iraq War, was greatly curtailed, as the Dixie Chicks discovered in 2003. Country music fans pilloried the singers for their comments about President Bush overseas. Thus, tolerance ebbs and flows depending on whether the country is at war, at peace, in an economic boom, or in a depression. These factors and others influence the level of freedom of expression over time and, hence, the meaning of the First Amendment.

Philosophical Justifications for Freedom of Expression

Freedom of expression is considered one of the most important of our protected rights. But just as judges and scholars have not always agreed on the meaning of the First Amendment, theorists do not always agree on why freedom of expression is important. Generally, the goal of First Amendment theorists is to explain why freedom of expression is so cherished and to set out the parameters of its protection. Theorists fall into two camps: those who argue that freedom of expression protects an important social value—self-governance—and those who argue it protects an important individual value—self-fulfillment. All theorists draw the line on protected speech somewhere; none are absolutists.

The types of expression that each theorist chooses to exclude from protection depend on what the theorist seeks to protect: society or the individual. An understanding of First Amendment theory is important for public relations professionals because it determines the level of protection public relations speech will receive.

Freedom of Expression as a Social Value

Freedom of expression has been seen as serving an important societal value in that it promotes democratic government, acts as a check on governmental abuses, facilitates peaceful change, and serves in the search for truth.[3] The social value theories usually apply to speech charged with a public purpose, not with a private or self-interested purpose. As will be seen, the Supreme Court has used the notion of freedom of expression as a social value to justify extending First Amendment protection to corporate speech, but not to commercial speech.

Freedom of Expression as an Individual Value

On the other side of the theoretical spectrum are those theorists who view freedom of expression as furthering the individual value of self-fulfillment or self-realization.[4] For these theorists, freedom of expression is a good in itself. The ability to communicate allows humans to realize their full potential and is one of the factors that separates them from animals. Therefore, freedom of speech is seen as being a benefit to the speaker as well as to the receiver of the information. The approach of the individualist theorists is more protective of commercial speech, and the U.S. Supreme Court has used this value to extend limited First Amendment protection to it.

Corporate Speech

Corporations, although artificial entities created by law, have many of the same rights as natural persons. They are, for example, entitled to equal protection and due process of the law.[5] But until fairly recently, corporations were not thought to have First Amendment rights because corporations cannot achieve the individual values of self-fulfillment or self-realization. Beginning in 1978, however, the U.S. Supreme Court came to recognize that corporations do contribute to public policy debates and that individuals have a First Amendment right to hear what corporations have to say on public issues. Thus the Court, in speech cases involving corporations, began looking at the social values that freedom of expression promotes, thereby paving the way for First Amendment protection of corporate speech.

Corporate speech is speech by corporations concerning political and social issues. The purpose of corporate speech is not to promote a product or service, but rather the corporation's views or position on a matter of public importance. Corporations may speak out on issues such as environmentalism to affect government policy or to build positive relationships with their stakeholders. Such speech falls squarely within the bailiwick of public relations, taking the form of brochures, pamphlets, issue/advocacy ads, or position papers, among other communication materials.

Protections for Corporate Speech

The first case in which corporate speech was recognized involved a Massachusetts law prohibiting a corporation from speaking on referendum proposals unless those proposals "materially affected its business, property, or assets."[6] The First National Bank of Boston challenged the law because it wanted to publicize its views on a proposed constitutional amendment that would have granted the state legislature the right to impose a graduated income tax on Massachusetts residents. First National opposed the amendment and sought to inform its customers of its position via a public relations campaign.

In denying the bank's claim, the lower court, taking an individualist approach, said the issue was whether corporations had First Amendment rights. The court concluded they did not, but the Supreme Court disagreed. Justice Lewis Powell, writing for the majority, said that the issue was not whether corporations had the same speech rights as natural persons, but whether the speech in question was protected by the First Amendment. In other words, the content of the speech determined the protection granted, not the nature of the speaker. The speech here, the Court said, was "the type of speech indispensable to decision-making [sic] in a democracy, and this is no less true because the speech comes from a corporation rather than an individual."[7]

Two years later, the Court reinforced its protection of corporate speech in *Consolidated Edison Co. v. Public Service Commission*.[8] In the case, the Public Service Commission of the State of New York had prohibited the inclusion of inserts discussing controversial issues of public policy in monthly electric bills. The prohibition came after Consolidated Edison had included in its January 1976 bills an insert titled "Independence is Still a Goal, and

Nuclear Power is Needed to Win the Battle." The insert presented Consolidated Edison's views on the benefits of nuclear power. In response, the Natural Resources Defense Council (NRDC), a nonprofit organization, requested that the company include a rebuttal prepared by NRDC in its next month's billing. When Consolidated Edison refused, the NRDC sought an order from the Public Service Commission forcing Consolidated Edison to include the rebuttal. The Public Service Commission refused to make that order but attempted to settle the matter by prohibiting any discussion of controversial public policy issues in utility bill inserts. Consolidated Edison challenged the prohibition.

The majority of the Supreme Court struck down the prohibition as an unconstitutional infringement on Consolidated Edison's First Amendment rights. Although the government could regulate the time, place, and manner of corporate speech, it could not do so on the basis of content. The government could not restrict speech on a topic simply because it might be offensive to some people, the Court held.

Nor can the government force a corporation to disseminate messages with which it disagrees. Under a California rule, the Public Utilities Commission of California had ordered Pacific Gas and Electric Company to include in its bills messages prepared by a consumer group opposing the company's rate increase requests. The Court held that corporations, like individuals, cannot be compelled to associate with views with which they do not agree.[9]

Restrictions on Corporate Speech

Critics of extending speech rights to corporations focus on the pervasive influence of corporations in society today. They argue that corporations have such wealth and power that their voices could drown out the speech of individuals and distort the debate on public policy issues.[10] Microsoft and Google, for example, have more money, more resources, and more clout than any one individual in today's society. If those companies decided to get involved in a political issue, those on the other side of the issue might not get the same media coverage and attention. This argument can be seen clearly in the corporate speech cases involving political campaigns and the election process. As the Supreme Court put it, "Regulation of corporate political activity thus has reflected concern not about the use of the corporate form per se, but about the potential for unfair deployment of wealth for political purposes."[11]

The Federal Election Campaign Act of 1971, for example, prohibits a corporation from using money from its general treasury fund to make a contribution or expenditure related to candidates for federal office. Contributions of money or services are made directly to a candidate or a candidate's campaign committee to be used at the discretion of the candidate. Expenditures are made independently of the candidate but in support of the campaign. The act's purpose is twofold. First, it prevents corporations from "buying" candidates through contributions made to their campaigns. Second, it protects corporate shareholders and employees from compelled speech. General treasury funds technically belong to the shareholders (the owners of the company) and are used in part to pay employees. By using those funds to support a political candidate, a corporation is forcing its shareholders and employees indirectly to subsidize the campaign of a candidate with whom they may disagree. Many states have enacted legislation similar to the Federal Election Campaign Act, thereby restricting the use of corporate treasury funds for political campaigns. In *Austin v. Michigan Chamber of Commerce*, the Supreme Court upheld the Michigan Campaign Finance Act prohibiting such activity.[12] The Michigan Chamber of Commerce challenged the section because it wanted to use treasury funds to place an ad in a local paper supporting a candidate for office. The Supreme Court upheld the Michigan act, stressing the "corrosive and distorting effects of immense aggregation of wealth that are accumulated with the help of the corporate form."[13] The section protects the small businesspersons who want to maintain membership in the Chamber of Commerce but who do not want their dues going to support political campaigns, the Court held.

The Court distinguished for-profit corporations from nonprofit, ideological organizations whose purpose is to promote a particular agenda. The Court had earlier held that Massachusetts Citizens for Life (MCL), a nonprofit corporation, could use treasury funds to promote the candidacy of particular politicians. In *FEC v. Massachusetts Citizens for Life, Inc.*, the Court held that because MCL's resources came from voluntary donations from people who supported its political agenda, there was no threat of compelled speech.[14] Contributors to MCL knew the ideology of the corporation and agreed with it.

In 2002, the Bipartisan Campaign Reform Act (BCRA) was enacted to close loopholes in the campaign-finance regulations that were disclosed by a 1998 Senate investigation into campaign practices.[15] Two practices in particular were seen as problematic because of their potential to influence federal elections: the use of soft money (defined as contributions for nonfederal, party-building activities) and the airing of issue ads (defined as political messages that did not expressly advocate the election or defeat of a specific candidate). Both practices were unregulated by the earlier Federal Election Campaign Act and had become increasingly popular during the 1990s. The BCRA prohibits soft money contributions to national political parties and prohibits broadcast advertising by unions and corporations or any organization using union and corporate funds within sixty days of a general election or thirty days of a primary or caucus if the ads refer to a candidate for federal election. Such issue ads are defined in the act as electioneering communications. The BCRA also bans corporate and union expenditures for electioneering from general treasuries.

State and federal campaign laws do not entirely prohibit corporations from participating in political campaigns. Corporations are free to set up separate accounts to finance campaigns. Under the federal law, these political action committees (PACs) can contribute a maximum of $5,000 to each candidate per election but can make unlimited expenditures on advertisements and other expenses that support a campaign. Individuals are subject to similar contribution limits to prevent the threat of corruption in the electoral process.

Commercial Speech

Although corporate speech on issues relating to political and social policies does receive First Amendment protection, speech related to a company's business may be considered commercial speech and subject to greater government regulation. Commercial speech has been defined by the Supreme Court as either speech that does "no more than propose a commercial transaction" or as expression "solely motivated by the desire for profit."[16]

Advertisements specifically promoting a product or service are not difficult to classify as commercial speech. They satisfy either definition used by the courts. But communication materials such as brochures and informational pamphlets are harder to classify. And the classification is important because commercial speech has less First Amendment protection from government regulation than corporate speech.

From a public relations perspective, the goal would be to have public relations materials considered corporate speech, warranting high protection from government regulation. Public relations campaigns are designed to foster relationships with publics, not to "sell" publics on the company's products or services. Therefore, restricting commercial speech to speech that does no more than propose a commercial transaction works to the public relations professional's advantage. But when the Court uses the economic motivation definition, a great deal of public relations speech falls under the commercial speech umbrella and becomes subject to regulation.

Unfortunately, the Supreme Court has not provided much guidance in how to determine whether speech by a corporation will be considered corporate or commercial speech. The only test enunciated by the Court to date comes from the 1983 case of *Bolger v. Youngs Drug Products Corp.*[17] Youngs Drug manufactured condoms. To promote its products, it sent unsolicited direct mail pieces to the general public. One piece was an informational pamphlet on the prevention of venereal disease through the use of condoms. At the end of the pamphlet, Youngs Drug's name appeared as the producer of the pamphlet. An action was brought against Youngs Drug because a federal postal regulation prohibited the mailing of unsolicited advertisements regarding contraception. Although it ultimately held that the postal regulation violated the First Amendment, the Supreme Court found that the informational pamphlet was commercial speech because:

- It was conceded to be an advertisement;
- It referred to specific products by Youngs Drug; and
- It was motivated by profit.

The three factors would not be sufficient individually to turn the informational pamphlet into commercial speech, but the combination of all three supported a finding that it was, the Court said. The Court was concerned that holding otherwise would lead advertisers to combine false or misleading product information with social or political information to avoid government regulation.

In 2003, the Court had an opportunity to clarify the commercial/corporate speech definitional issue when it initially agreed to hear an appeal from a California ruling in *Kasky v. Nike, Inc.* Relying heavily on the Supreme Court's decision in *Youngs Drug,* the California Supreme Court had held that Nike's efforts to refute allegations that its foreign factories were sweatshops constituted commercial, not corporate, speech and were therefore subject to state laws prohibiting false and misleading advertising.[18] Nike had sought to counter the allegations concerning its labor practices by issuing statements defending its record in "press releases, in letters to newspapers, in a letter to university presidents and athletic directors, and in other documents distributed for public relations purposes."[19] According to the court, Nike's messages were commercial speech because they "were directed by a commercial speaker to a commercial audience, and because they made representations of fact about the speaker's own business operations for the purpose of promoting sales of its products."[20] The court held that to determine whether a company's speech was commercial, the following factors had to be considered:

- **Speaker.** Was the speaker engaged in commerce?
- **Intended audience.** Was the intended audience the actual or potential buyers of the speaker's goods or services, or those likely to repeat the message to buyers?
- **Content of message.** Was the message commercial in nature (representing facts about the business operations, products, or services for the purpose of promoting sales)?

The U.S. Supreme Court chose ultimately not to hear the appeal on the basis that the case was before it too early in the litigation process and sent it back for trial. Nike, however, settled the case, agreeing to pay $1.5 million to the Fair Labor Association. The result is that the California decision stands as the law in that state. The court's opinion should serve as a reminder to public relations professionals that their efforts may well be considered commercial speech and subject to government regulation.

The Commercial Speech Doctrine

The concept of commercial speech in First Amendment law is a recent one. Advertising was unregulated by the government until the beginning of the twentieth century. In 1914, the Federal Trade Commission (FTC) was set up to protect businesses from one another. The idea was to protect competition by keeping businesses from using misleading ads to steal customers away from competitors. During the second half of the twentieth century, however, the emphasis shifted to the protection of the consumer.

The Supreme Court first considered whether the First Amendment protected commercial speech in 1942. The case arose when F. J. Chrestensen advertised tours of his surplus U.S.

Navy submarine by handing out leaflets.[21] New York City's sanitary code, however, prohibited the distribution of leaflets on city streets. Only handbills dedicated to information or public protest could be distributed. Threatened with charges under the sanitary code, Chrestensen printed a protest of the code's ban on the back of his ad. Although clever, the scheme did not save him from being charged and convicted. He appealed his conviction all the way to the Supreme Court.

The Court was not sympathetic to Chrestensen's plight, holding that "purely commercial advertising" was outside the gambit of the First Amendment. First, the justices said that he had added his protest just to get around the law. They did not buy his argument that the protest made it political speech. Second, although the government was limited in the restraints it could impose on the use of public streets for the dissemination of information and ideas, the Constitution imposed no such restraints on government with respect to purely commercial speech. Commercial speech was simply not as valuable to society, the Court held, as was political speech, and therefore it should not be protected.

In subsequent cases, the Court clarified its reasons for denying First Amendment protection to commercial speech. First, the Court was not worried about the chilling effect of regulation on commercial speech. One of the Court's primary justifications for protecting political speech—speech critical of the government—is the fear that people would stop speaking out against the government if they could be punished by the government for so doing. But ads, according to the Court, would continue regardless of whether they were protected by the First Amendment because the desire of businesses to make a profit is so strong. Second, the Court concluded that it was easier to determine whether an ad's claims were true than it was to determine whether allegations against the government were true. Therefore, while society had to tolerate a certain level of false political speech to ensure that political speech continued, society did not have to tolerate false ads.

Starting in the 1960s, however, the Court began to whittle away at the notion that commercial speech had no First Amendment protection. The movement toward protection for commercial speech coincided with the rise of consumerism. The case to start the process was *New York Times v. Sullivan*.[22] Although known primarily as a landmark libel case, it involved an editorial ad. The Court in *Sullivan* said that because of the nature of the ad—it dealt with political speech—it should be granted First Amendment protection. The Court distinguished between purely commercial advertising and political advertising, carving out an area of commercial speech that had First Amendment protection.

The Supreme Court moved closer to protecting commercial speech in *Bigelow v. Virginia*, a 1975 case.[23] An editor of a Virginia newspaper had accepted an ad that said low-cost abortions were available in New York state. A Virginia statute prohibited the circulation of publications encouraging the procurement of abortions. The Court held that ads for abortion referral services were not "purely commercial." They contained important factual information clearly of interest to members of the public. The Court concluded, essentially, that speech was not necessarily denied First Amendment protection simply because it appeared in the form of an advertisement.

The Court continued its expansion of protection for commercial speech the next year in *Virginia State Board of Pharmacy v. Virginia Citizens Consumer Council*.[24] The Virginia code prohibited pharmacists from advertising prices for prescription drugs. The idea was that an aggressive price war among pharmacies would ultimately hurt the consumer because consumers should choose pharmacists based on trust and understanding, not on the cost of drugs. A consumer group brought an action to force the state to change the code, arguing that the price of prescription drugs was important information for consumers.

The Court agreed and held that commercial speech can be as important to people as political speech, especially in terms of their everyday lives. In keeping with the new emphasis on the consumer, the Court emphasized the right of the consumer to have access to information, rather than the right of the pharmacists to advertise. It was the communication itself that was protected by the First Amendment, not the speaker. The Court did say, however, that advertising restrictions unrelated to content might be permissible.

A few years later, the Court set out a test for determining whether such a restriction was permissible. The case, *Central Hudson Gas & Electric Corp. v. Public Service Commission*, arose when a utility company challenged a regulation banning promotional advertising encouraging the consumption of electricity.[25] The Court overturned the regulation, holding that a total ban on ads touting electricity consumption violated the First Amendment.

The Court then devised a four-part test for courts to apply in determining whether a regulation is permissible. Under the test, courts must consider each of the following:

- whether the commercial speech is worthy of First Amendment protection;
- whether the government has a substantial interest for regulating the speech;
- whether the regulation in question directly advances the government's interest; and
- whether the regulation is no broader than necessary to realize that interest.

Commercial Speech Worthy of Protection

The first part of the *Central Hudson* test is a threshold test that must be met by the advertiser. The speech must be commercial speech that is accurate and for a lawful product or service. False and misleading ads and ads for illegal products or services are not eligible for First Amendment protection.

Substantial Government Interest

Assuming the commercial speech is accurate and for a lawful product, the burden of proof shifts to the government, which must meet each of the last three prongs of the *Central Hudson* test. The first thing the government must show is that it has a substantial interest in regulating the commercial speech. Usually, courts consider the government to have a substantial interest in protecting "the health, safety, morals and aesthetic quality of the community."[26]

In *Posadas de Puerto Rico Associates v. Tourism Company of Puerto Rico*,[27] for example, the Puerto Rican government argued that it restricted the advertising of casinos because it wanted to protect its citizens from the evils of gambling. To promote tourism, advertising the casinos in the United States was permitted; but such advertising was banned on the island itself. After finding that the advertising was for a legal activity and not misleading, the Court held that Puerto Rico's interest in reducing gambling by Puerto Rican residents was substantial because the legislature sought to prevent the cultural and moral evils that accompany casino gambling.

Direct Advancement of Interest

The third prong of the *Central Hudson* test requires that the government establish that its restriction would directly advance the interest it is protecting. In *Posadas*, the Court held that the third prong was satisfied simply because it was reasonable to make the assumption that advertising would increase the demand for casino gambling. In recent cases, however, the Court has begun to require more in the way of evidence from the government to support its contention that the restriction directly advances its interest. In *Rubin v. Coors Brewing Co.*, Coors sought to state the alcohol content on its bottles of beer.[28] The government said that stating the alcohol content on labels would cause a brewing war among beer producers. Coors argued in return that wine and liquor manufacturers are required to have the alcohol content on their labels, and there has never been a strength war with those spirits. This time the Court asked for empirical evidence that listing the alcohol content on a beer label would in fact cause a strength war.

The positive trend was continued with another liquor advertising case. The *44 Liquormart v. Rhode Island* case began with a challenge to a Rhode Island statute banning liquor stores from off-premises advertising of their prices.[29] The state's justification for the ban was that it would prevent price competition among liquor retailers, thus keeping the prices artificially high and promoting temperance among the state's citizens. Higher prices, the government argued, meant less alcohol consumption. Retailer 44 Liquormart challenged the law after the state fined the store for a newspaper ad that did not explicitly state the price of its liquor products but instead used the word "wow" to suggest low prices.

The Supreme Court unanimously struck down the ban, although the justices varied on their reasons for so doing. The Court noted that commercial speech had been an important form of communication since before the nation's founding. It also noted that not all advertising was subject to the same standard of review merely because of its status as commercial speech. Government regulation that was designed to protect the consumer from misleading, deceptive, or aggressive sales practices would be subject to less rigorous First Amendment review. In this case, the Court found that the state simply had not proved that increased prices would significantly reduce consumption. In fact, the evidence suggested that heavy drinkers would be undeterred by the higher prices. So the ban failed the advancement prong of *Central Hudson*.

No Broader than Necessary

Even if the government can show that its restriction directly advances its interests, it still must establish that the regulation is no broader than necessary. In other words, it must not restrict more commercial speech than it needs to. In *Posadas*, the Court held that the ban on casino advertising was actually quite narrow, since it applied only to advertising aimed at residents, not tourists. The Court went on to note that since gambling could be banned altogether, the lesser action of banning domestic advertising was constitutionally permissible. The dissenting justices argued that there were other, less restrictive means available for the government to protect its citizens from gambling, including advertising the evils of it.

The Court returned to the issue of the fourth part of the test in *Board of Trustees of the State University of New York v. Fox*, a 1989 case.[30] A Tupperware party in a college dorm had been advertised at State University of New York. The board of trustees, however, had said that there was to be no commercial activity in dorms. The university wanted to protect the students from commercial exploitation and to create an educational atmosphere. The Court altered the fourth part of the *Central Hudson* test from "no broader than necessary to realize the government's interest" to "a reasonable fit between the regulation and the government interest." On that reading, the Tupperware party was properly banned.

The Court also rejected the argument in *Posadas* that because the government had the right to ban the activity, it had the right to ban the advertising of that activity. The Court said that banning speech may actually have more impact than banning the activity and that under the First Amendment, speech is given greater protection than conduct. The Court reinforced that position when it struck down provisions of the Food and Drug Administration Modernization Act that precluded pharmacists from advertising compounded drugs. While acknowledging that protecting the integrity of the FDA's drug approval process was a substantial interest, the Court in *Thompson v. Western States Medical Center* held that the interest could have been advanced by other means that did not include restrictions on speech.[31]

Specific Areas of Commercial Speech

Although the Court applies the *Central Hudson* test to all commercial speech cases, it reaches different decisions depending on the kind of product or service advertised. For example, in *Greater New Orleans Broadcasting Association v. United States,* the Court strongly supported the right of truthful, nondeceptive advertising, even of "vice" products and services (such as alcohol, tobacco, and gambling), to protection under the First Amendment.[32] Yet, the Court has consistently limited the advertising of professionals, such as lawyers, accountants, and dentists. Professionals may advertise the price of standardized procedures but not of more complex services.[33] The Court has also restricted the means by which lawyers may communicate with consumers.[34]

Summary

The guiding principle of modern First Amendment law has been the notion that government cannot limit expression based on the content of the speech or the identity of the speaker. The Supreme Court has determined that corporations have important contributions to make in public debates and the content of such speech should be protected. At the same time, however, restrictions on that speech are permissible to avoid the potential for corruption, especially in the election process, and to protect corporate investors and employees. Commercial speech, which does no more than propose a commercial transaction or is solely motivated by the desire for profit, receives less First Amendment protection than corporate speech. Communications coming out of public relations departments or agencies may be considered commercial speech, especially if directed to consumers.

Discussion Questions

1. Define corporate speech and commercial speech. What values has the Supreme Court sought to protect by extending First Amendment protection to each category of speech?

2. What are the arguments against extending First Amendment protection to corporate speech? What are the arguments for protecting corporate speech? How do the ethical standards of business, such as profit maximization and social responsibility, play into the arguments for and against?

3. Using the California court's test in *Kasky v. Nike*, under what situations, if any, would a company's speech be considered corporate rather than commercial?

4. You are the public relations director for a small liberal arts university. Recently there have been some fights in campus dorms involving drunk students. The university is concerned about the number of students who are drinking and how their behavior is affecting the school's image. The university wants to ask the city council to pass an ordinance prohibiting the use of a billboard on the edge of campus to advertise local drinking establishments. In other words, the ordinance would ban the advertising of bars on billboards. How might you advise the school's president about the legal status of such an ordinance?

Notes

[1] William Blackstone, *Commentaries on the Laws of England*, ed. H. Broom and E. A. Hadley (Holmes Beach, FL: Gaunt, 1999. Original work published in 1869), 151.

[2] See, for example, Lawrence Levy, *Emergence of a Free Press* (New York: Oxford University Press, 1985).

[3] Alexander Meiklejohn, *Free Speech and Its Relations to Self-government* (Port Washington, NY: Kennikat, 1948); Thomas Emerson, *Toward a General Theory of the First Amendment* (New York: Random House, 1966).

[4] Ibid. Martin Redish, *Freedom of Expression: A Critical Analysis* (Charlottesville, VA: Michie, 1984).

[5] *Santa Clara County v. Southern Pacific R.R.*, 118 U.S. 394 (1996); *Smyth v. Ames*, 169 U.S. 466 (1898).

[6] *First National Bank of Boston v. Bellotti*, 435 U.S. 765 (1978).

[7] Ibid., 777.

[8] *Consolidated Edison Co. v. Public Service Commission*, 447 U.S. 530 (1980).

[9] *Pacific Gas & Electric Co. v. Public Utilities Commission of California*, 475 U.S. 1 (1986).

[10] *First National Bank*, 435 U.S. (1978).

[11] *FEC v. Massachusetts Citizens for Life, Inc.*, 479 U.S. 238, 257 (1986).

[12] *Austin v. Michigan Chamber of Commerce*, 494 U.S. 652 (1990).

[13] Ibid., 660.

[14] *FEC v. Massachusetts*.

[15] Bipartisan Campaign Reform Act. 116 Stat. 81 (2002).

[16] *Pittsburgh Press Co. v. Pittsburgh Commission on Human Relations et al.*, 413 U.S. 376, 385 (1973); *Dun & Bradstreet v. Greenmoss Builders, Inc.*, 472 U.S. 749, 762 (1985).

[17] *Bolger v. Youngs Drug Products Corp.*, 463 U.S. 60 (1983).

[18] *Kasky v. Nike, Inc.*, 27 Cal. 4th 939 (2002).

[19] Ibid.

[20] Ibid.

[21] *Valentine v. Chrestensen*, 316 U.S. 52 (1942).

[22] *New York Times v. Sullivan*, 376 U.S. 254 (1964).

[23] *Bigelow v. Virginia*, 421 U.S. 809 (1975).

[24] *Virginia State Board of Pharmacy v. Virginia Citizens Consumer Council*, 425 U.S. 748 (1976).

[25] *Central Hudson Gas & Electric Corp. v. Public Service Commission*, 447 U.S. 577 (1980).

[26] Ken Middleton, B. Chamberlin, and Matthew Bunker, *The Law of Public Communication*, 4th ed. (New York: Longman, 1997), 309.

[27] *Posadas de Puerto Rico Associates v. Tourism Company of Puerto Rico*, 478 U.S. 328 (1986).

[28] *Rubin v. Coors Brewing Co.*, 514 U.S. 476 (1995).

[29] *44 Liquormart v. Rhode Island*, 517 U.S. 484 (1996).

[30] *Board of Trustees of the State University of New York v. Fox*, 492 U.S. 469 (1989).

[31] *Thompson v. Western States Medical Center*, 535 U.S. 357 (2002).

[32] *Greater New Orleans Broadcasting Association v. United States*, 119 S. Ct. 1923 (1999).

[33] *Bates v. State Bar of Arizona*, 433 U.S. 350 (1977); *California Dental Ass'n v. FTC*, No. 97-1625, *slip op.* (U.S. May 24, 1999).

[34] *Went For It, Inc. v. The Florida Bar*, 115 S. Ct. 2371 (1995).

chapter three

REGULATING PUBLIC RELATIONS SPEECH

Public relations professionals must be aware of the various governmental regulations and agencies affecting their organization's or client's business. Although each industry has its own agencies and regulations with which it needs to be concerned, those most often affecting public relations will be discussed here. Failure to understand these regulations opens up public relations professionals and their organizations to liability for breaching them.

Lobbying

The First Amendment gives individuals the right to free speech and also to petition the government for redress of grievances. Both of these rights come into play with lobbying. Lobbying is carried out through direct contact with legislators or through indirect public relations campaigns. Although lobbying is protected by the First Amendment, the government is permitted to regulate it to prevent corruption of the democratic process.

Lobbying is controlled by the Lobbying Disclosure Act of 1995.[1] The act defines lobbyists as individuals who make more than one contact on behalf of a client and spend at least 20 percent of their time during a six-month period providing that service to the client. A contact is defined as "a communication, either oral or written, on behalf of a client to a covered executive or legislative branch official regarding legislation, rules, regulations, grants, loans, permits, programs or the nomination of anyone subject to Senate confirmation."[2] Grassroots lobbying—

using a public relations campaign to influence public opinion about an issue with the goal of influencing government policy on the issue—is not generally considered lobbying for the purposes of the act.

Each state has its own guidelines for defining and registering lobbyists. Generally, in-house lobbyists are the permanent employees of an organization who manage that group's lobbying efforts; whereas lobbyists can support one or more clients on a contract basis based on their affiliations or type of service provided.

Lobbyists who make more than $5,000 in a six-month period for their services and in-house lobbyists who expect to spend more than $20,000 on lobbying activities in a six-month period must register with the federal government. Registered lobbyists are required to file statements identifying their client and detailing the general areas and specific issues on which they have lobbied.[3]

Lobbyists who work for foreign clients are also to disclose their activities. Prior to World War II, Congress became concerned with the distribution of pro-German and communist literature in the United States. To control this "un-American propaganda," as it was termed, Congress passed the Foreign Agents Registration Act of 1938.[4] Under the act and its amendments, foreign agents must report their affiliations, the way they carry out their activities, and how they disseminate information to influence American public opinion. They also must attach the label "political propaganda" to any material disseminated by them.

A foreign agent includes any American who acts "as a public relations counsel, publicity agent, information-service employee or political consultant" for a foreign client. As of 1996, only agents who work for foreign governments are required to register under the Foreign Agents Registration Act.[5] Those who work for foreign companies and trade associations must register under the Lobbying Disclosure Act.

Federal Trade Commission

Commercial speech can be regulated at both the federal and state levels, but the primary regulatory body is the Federal Trade Commission (FTC). Congress established the FTC in 1914 to police unfair methods of business competition. Its original concern was the impact of advertising on competitors, not consumers. That has changed over the years, and today it is primarily concerned with commercial speech that misleads the public. Its most important responsibility is to ensure that consumers are not taken advantage of by unfair or deceptive advertising.[6] The FTC takes a broad view of advertising, including within the term public relations materials as well.

Unfairness

In 1994, Congress defined an unfair act or practice as one that "causes or is likely to cause substantial injury to consumers which is not reasonably avoidable by consumers themselves and not outweighed by countervailing benefits to consumers or to competition."[7] Unfairness more often arises in the treatment of customers than in advertisements. Substantial injury usually involves monetary losses, although it includes physical harm.[8]

Deceptive Advertising

The FTC defines deceptive advertising as a material representation, omission, or practice that is likely to mislead a reasonable consumer.[9]

Material Representation or Omission

The FTC says the representation, omission, or practice must be material. Express claims as to the attributes of a product are always considered material. Ads involving health and safety are usually presumed to be material, as are those containing information that pertains to the central characteristic of the product. An example is an ad for Rapid Shave by Colgate-Palmolive in which it was claimed that the product was so good that it could be used to shave sandpaper.[10] In a TV demonstration, Rapid Shave was spread on sandpaper and then a few seconds later was shaved off. The problem was, it was not sandpaper. It was sand sprinkled on glass. The FTC complained that the ad was deceptive and a material misrepresentation that could affect a consumer's decision to purchase the product. Colgate-Palmolive argued that the product really could shave sandpaper if left on long enough but that on TV, sand and paper were the same color. To get the proper visual impression, glass had to be used. The Supreme Court agreed with the FTC that this was a material misrepresentation.

Not all mock-ups or fake demonstrations are misleading. Only those used to support a material product claim must be restricted. A fake TV, for example, could be used in an ad for TV stands because no claim about the quality of the TV is being made. A fake TV could not be used to advertise the TV itself, especially if the ad were extolling the virtues of the sharp, clear quality of the screen image.

Likely to Mislead

The likelihood of an advertisement to mislead or cause deception is sufficient for it to be considered deceptive. A deceptive statement may mislead expressly (e.g., "Using Listerine prevents colds") or by implication (the ad suggests that the product contains certain elements or does certain things).[11] The omission of important or material information can also make an ad deceptive. For example, an unsolicited direct mail letter from Peoples Credit First told recipients they had been approved for "a Peoples Credit First platinum card with a credit line of $5,000.00."[12] To receive what recipients believed to be a Visa or MasterCard credit card, recipients had to sign the acceptance certificate and remit a one-time-only fee of $45. What they actually received, however, was a membership package that included a merchandise catalogue, a brochure, and a platinum-colored card with the recipient's name and an account number. A district court found that Peoples had expressly represented that the consumer would receive a platinum credit card with a $5,000 credit limit. Peoples argued that the words "credit" and "card" never actually appeared together in the letter and that the fee was specifically referred to as a "membership" fee. In rejecting that argument, the court noted that while the representation was technically true, it must be viewed as a whole when considering whether it was likely to mislead a reasonable consumer. The letter left the impression that the consumer would receive a credit card.

Reasonable Consumer

When reviewing an advertisement, the FTC considers it from the perspective of a reasonable consumer. The test is whether a consumer's interpretation or reaction to an ad is reasonable.[13] When ads are targeted to a specific audience, such as the elderly, then the test will be how a reasonable member of that group reacts. Advertisers are not responsible for every possible interpretation or behavior of a consumer. The law is not designed to protect the foolish or the feebleminded, for example. The FTC acknowledges that some people, because of ignorance or incomprehension, may be misled by even an honest claim.

Substantiation

Advertisers must have a reasonable basis for making their claims and must be able to substantiate those claims with scientific studies. The FTC originated the substantiation requirement in a ruling involving Pfizer Pharmaceutical. The FTC ruled that because the company could produce no scientific evidence to support the claim that its Unburn suntan lotion "actually anesthetizes nerves" to relieve pain, it had no reasonable basis for so claiming.[14]

The most recent policy guidelines on substantiation were released in 1984.[15] They provide that express substantiation claims, such as "doctors recommend" and "specific tests prove," require the level of proof advertised. Otherwise, advertisers will be expected to have at least a reasonable basis for the claims in their ads. The degree of substantiation that will be deemed reasonable varies depending on the type of claim, the product, and the consequences of a false claim. The major effect of substantiation has been to shift the burden of proof from the FTC, which previously had to prove the ad was false, to the advertiser, who now has to prove the ad is true. If the case goes to court, however, the burden shifts back to the FTC to prove the ad is misleading or false.

In 2005, the FTC filed a complaint in district court against the marketers of the weight-loss supplement Xenadrine EFX for making false and unsubstantiated claims about the product.[16] Studies commissioned by the marketers showed that subjects taking Xenadrine EFX lost an average of only 1.5 pounds over a 10-week period, while those taking a placebo lost an average of 2.5 pounds over the same period. Despite that finding, Xenadrine EFX was advertised as clinically proven to cause rapid and substantial weight loss.

Substantiation applies not only to advertisements, but also to public relations materials that may include claims from scientific studies. It is the public relations professional preparing the material whom the FTC will require to substantiate the claim. Therefore, it is imperative that public relations professionals personally see any surveys or evidence before including questionable claims in promotional materials. A survey or study paid for by the client cannot, for example, be described as an "independent" study.

Fine Print

Small print at the bottom of an ad will not necessarily save the ad because the FTC does not believe the average consumer reads the fine print. In 1994, for example, the FTC ruled that Häagen-Dazs frozen yogurt ads were false and misleading.[17] The ads claimed the yogurt bars were low fat, or 98 percent fat free. That description actually fit only two of the nine flavors. The company claimed that each ad had a disclaimer in fine print that said the "98 percent fat free" statement referred to only certain flavors. The disclaimer was not sufficient to protect the company.

Insignificant Facts

Advertisers may not state insignificant facts in such a way that they appear significant. For example, the claim that "Gaines-burgers dog food provides all the milk protein a dog needs" was misleading because dogs do not need milk protein.[18] Another example was an ad for Wonder Bread that said the bread was fortified with vitamins and minerals to help children grow up big and strong.[19] What the company failed to say was that almost all commercially baked bread is fortified with vitamins and minerals. Wonder Bread was no different in that respect from any other bread. In both cases, insignificant facts were made to appear significant.

Puffery

The FTC does not pursue subjective claims based on taste, smell, appearance, or feel. These claims are called puffery and are believed to have no effect on consumers. An example would be a Coca-Cola ad claiming Coke is the most refreshing drink around. Nor is the FTC greatly concerned with ads for products or services that consumers can easily evaluate, that are inexpensive, or that are frequently purchased.

Testimonials and Endorsements

Product endorsements have grown dramatically in popularity over the years. These include infomercials that often feature celebrities and the "man on the street" testimonials. The FTC has defined an endorsement or testimonial as an ad that consumers are likely to believe reflects the opinion, beliefs, findings, or experience of a party other than the sponsoring advertiser.[20] It is sometimes difficult to determine when an actor is endorsing a product or simply playing a role. Testimonials using typical consumers must use typical consumers, not actors. And testimonials must reflect actual experiences. In the Xenadrine EFX case cited above, the consumers testifying in the ads about how much weight they had lost by taking Xenadrine EFX had actually engaged in rigorous diet and/or exercise programs. The ads also failed to disclose that the consumer endorsers were paid between $1,000 and $20,000 for their testimonials.[21]

A celebrity or expert endorser must be a bona fide user of the product at the time of the endorsement. This means the individual must use the product more than once in a while. And endorsers must use a product because they like it, not because they were given a year's supply.[22] Celebrity endorsements must also reveal a material connection between the endorser and the product if one exists. Entertainer Pat Boone was fined by the FTC for failing to meet this rule when he endorsed an acne medication.[23] In the ad, he implied that each of his four daughters had used the preparation successfully, a claim that was not completely true. He also failed to mention in the ad that one of his companies was promoting the product and that he received 25 cents for each bottle of the product sold.

FTC Remedies

If the FTC decides an ad is deceptive, the agency has a number of remedies at its disposal. One problem the FTC faces with advertising is that an ad campaign can be over long before the FTC catches up with the company and brings a complaint against it. On the other hand, what the FTC has going in its favor is the threat of publicity. Companies do not like the publicity that comes with a charge of false advertising, so publicity can be an effective sanction.

Prospective Remedies

The FTC issues staff opinion letters, advisory opinions, industry guidelines, and trade regulation rules that keep advertisers aware of what the FTC will consider deceptive.[24] For example, the FTC has outlined when a product can be described as "low fat" or "high fiber."[25] These guidelines help advertisers stay out of trouble.

Consent Decrees

When the FTC contacts a company about what the commission perceives as a deceptive ad campaign, the company can choose to voluntarily withdraw the ad and agree not to make the claim again. The FTC can persist, however, and request that the company sign a consent order that requires the company to promise to stop the ad and reimburse consumers who were misled by the ad. For example, the marketers of Xenadrine EFX signed a consent order with the FTC that required them to pay the FTC $100,000 and refrain from claiming that any weight-loss product causes permanent weight loss or that weight loss can occur without diet or exercise unless they had competent and reliable scientific evidence to substantiate the claims.[26] Failure to sign a consent order results in a hearing before an administrative law judge. The FTC can also seek an injunction to force the company to stop the ads.

Corrective Advertising

On occasion, the FTC will require a company to correct its advertising message. The basis for this remedy is that if a campaign has been long running and successful, a residue of misleading information remains in the mind of the public even after the misleading ads are removed. Under the corrective advertising remedy, the FTC forces the advertiser to inform the public that it has not been honest or has been misleading.

The first corrective advertising case came in 1971. ITT Continental Baking Company had been advertising that its Profile bread contained fewer calories than other bread and that eating it could help someone lose weight.[27] In fact, Profile had about the same number of calories per ounce as other bread, but it had seven fewer calories per slice because it was sliced thinner than other brands. Eating Profile would not cause someone to lose weight. The FTC forced the company to correct that impression. The company did so by having a then-well-known actress, Julia Meade, talk about how she, as a mother, would like to clear up any misunderstanding consumers might have about Profile bread. She explained the difference in the amount of calories and noted that although eating Profile would not actually cause someone to lose weight, it would help them achieve a balanced meal. While advertisers see corrective advertising as a harsh remedy—one commentator even described the scheme as "commercial hara-kiri"—studies have shown that most consumers do not see the ads as corrective at all.[28] They see them as just another ad for the product.[29]

Affirmative Disclosure

Corrective advertising is similar to affirmative disclosure, in which the advertiser is forced to include certain information in an ad. The classic example of affirmative disclosure is the Surgeon General's warning on cigarette packs. In April 2000, two manufacturers of natural and herbal cigarettes agreed to stop using ads that claimed their products were safer than their additive-rich tobacco competitors' products. The FTC charged that the smoke from these natural tobacco and herbal cigarettes contained levels of carcinogens and toxins similar to those found in cigarettes that include additives. In the settlement, the companies agreed to label their packages with the warning, "No additives in our tobacco does not mean a safer cigarette."[30]

Defenses

The basic defense against any false advertising complaint is truth, that is, proving that a product does what the ad says it does, that it is made where the ad says it is made, or that it is as beneficial as the ad says it is. In court, the burden is on the government to prove the ad is deceptive or misleading. The advertiser can also try to show that any statement in question is not material to the ad as a whole or that the ad does not imply what the government says it implies.

Agency Liability

Agencies preparing ads or public relations materials for their clients may be found liable for any deception. In determining whether an ad or public relations agency is liable for the misleading or deceptive ad, the FTC and the courts consider:

- whether the agency knew or should have known of the deceptive nature of the ad; and
- the extent and nature of the agency's participation in the creation of ad.[31]

Food and Drug Administration

The Food and Drug Administration (FDA) is concerned with the promotion of prescription drugs through the mass media, whether via advertising or public relations activities. The federal Food, Drug and Cosmetic Act defines a prescription drug as a drug "not safe for [human] use except under the supervision of a licensed practitioner."[32] As policy, the FDA labels all new drugs "prescription drugs," thereby requiring the supervision of a medical doctor until the drug is proved safe for consumers.[33]

The FDA has the jurisdiction to regulate "labels and any written, printed, or graphic matter" related to prescription drugs.[34] Courts have held that brochures and pamphlets promoting the product need not directly accompany a drug to be considered part of the drug's label. Making claims that have not been approved by the FDA can result in the FDA declaring the drug a "new drug" and subject to a physician's control.

In addition, the agency has set out guidelines for video, audio, and print releases about drugs. Releases must:

- provide a "fair balance" by telling consumers the benefits and the risks in taking the medicine;
- be clear about the limitations of the drug—in other words, the release must acknowledge that the drug will not help everyone; and
- be accompanied by supplementary information, such as brochures and pamphlets, that give the full prescribing information.

The Food, Drug and Cosmetic Act gives the FDA the power to seek injunctive relief, seize offending products, and issue criminal penalties. The FDA can also require companies to undertake corrective advertising. In 2003, the FDA determined that ads run by Bristol-Myers Squibb for Pravachol, a cholesterol-lowering drug, were misleading.[35] According to the FDA, the statement, "Pravachol is the only cholesterol lowering drug proven to help prevent first and second heart attack and stroke in people with high cholesterol or heart disease," suggested that Pravachol had been proven to help prevent stroke in people without heart disease. Bristol-Myers Squibb was forced to run an ad that corrected that impression. The ad included this statement: "Please note, Pravachol has *not* been proven to help prevent stroke in people *without* heart disease. Pravachol is proven to help prevent stroke only in people with coronary heart disease (CHD)."[36]

In March 2000, the Supreme Court ruled that the FDA lacked authority to regulate tobacco products.[37] The FDA had sought to bring tobacco under its jurisdiction. If tobacco were considered a drug for the purposes of the Food, Drug and Cosmetic Act, the FDA would have the authority to limit the amount of harmful chemicals in tobacco products. But the Court found that tobacco did not qualify as a drug or medical device under the act. Congress, the Court held, had never given the FDA the power to regulate tobacco; and until 1996, the FDA itself had denied it had the jurisdiction to do so. The ruling, while closing off FDA regulation for the time being, opened the door for state regulation of tobacco.

The Securities and Exchange Commission

The Securities and Exchange Commission (SEC), which oversees U.S. financial markets, grew out of the stock market crash that triggered the Great Depression. Congress passed the Securities Act of 1933 and the Securities Exchange Act of 1934 to monitor the financial affairs of publicly traded companies. The SEC was created by the 1934 act to "administer federal securities laws and issue rules and regulations to provide protection for investors and ensure that the securities markets are fair and honest."[38] Essentially, the purpose of the SEC is to ensure a level playing field for all investors by requiring truthful, complete, and timely disclosure of information about publicly traded companies that could be important to an investor's decision to buy, sell, or hold securities.

The Securities Act of 1933

The 1933 act, also called the Truth in Securities Act, deals with issues regarding new stocks and has two basic objectives: (1) to provide investors with material information concerning securities offered for sale to the public and (2) to prohibit misrepresentation, deceit, and other fraudulent acts and practices in the sale of securities generally.[39] The act requires that, before any security may be offered for sale to the public, a registration statement that discloses financial and other information about the issuing company (unless the company is exempt from registration) be filed with the SEC.

Prior to the filing of the registration statement, no press releases, news conferences, or other mass media publicity (including advertisements or promotions) encouraging the sale of the new securities are permitted. After the filing, there is a twenty-day waiting period during which time the company may issue a prospectus to a potential investor setting out financial information, but no actual offers to buy can be accepted. The SEC does permit tombstone ads during this period. Tombstone ads are text-based ads that simply identify the company, the number of securities to be issued, and other descriptive information. No graphics or persuasive techniques are permitted.

In a 1958 case, a brokerage house argued that its press release touting the virtues of a company about to make an initial public offering was "news" and therefore not subject to the restraint against advertising.[40] The SEC disagreed, claiming that "astute public relations activities" had "created" the news and that such activities were "precisely the evil which the Securities Act seeks to prevent."[41]

Section 11 of the act imposes liability on those who have included any untrue statement of a material fact in the registration statement or who have omitted any material fact from it. Material facts are those that would affect a reasonable investor's decision to buy the securities. Liability is imposed not only on the issuer, but also on the individuals who prepared the registration statement.

The Securities Exchange Act of 1934

The Securities Exchange Act of 1934 extends protection to investors trading in securities that are already issued and outstanding.[42] The act also imposes disclosure requirements on publicly held corporations and regulates tender offers and proxy solicitations.

The act's purposes are to ensure full disclosure of timely and pertinent information and to prevent any deception or manipulation of prices. To accomplish this, the SEC requires periodic reports to be filed detailing the financial state of a company, its future plans, and other information that could affect an investor's decision regarding that company's securities.

Annual Reports

The best-known financial report is the 10-K. Companies are required to file with the SEC a Form 10-K annually. In it, a company discloses specific information about its financial status and direction. That information forms the basis of the annual report that must be given to shareholders no less than fifteen days before the company's annual meeting. The SEC requirements for annual reports include:

- audited financial statements;
- supplementary financial information, such as net sales and gross profits;
- management discussion and analysis of financial condition;
- brief description of the company's business;
- names of the directors and officers; and
- description of any litigation in which the company or its directors are involved.

In addition, the SEC requires that annual reports be written in plain English so that investors can understand the information. Public relations professionals are often involved in writing the narrative portion of annual reports, including the letter to the shareholders from the president/CEO, and therefore need to be aware of the SEC rules to avoid liability.

Timely Disclosure

Section 10(b) of the 1934 act prohibits "any act, practice, or course of business which operates or would operate as a fraud or deceit upon any person, in connection with the purchase or sale of any security." Under SEC Rule 10b-5, it is deceptive or fraudulent for anyone "to make any untrue statements of a material fact or to omit to state a material fact." Although the SEC consistently refuses to define the word *material*, courts have treated information as material if it is likely to affect a reasonable investor's decision to buy, sell, or hold shares. Together, the section and rule require timely and accurate disclosure of material facts, which was the central issue in the 1968 landmark case involving the Texas Gulf Sulphur Company.

The case arose from a press release issued by Texas Gulf Sulphur on April 12, 1964, to squelch rumors that it had found one of the world's largest copper mines.[43] In the release, which was prepared with the help of a public relations agency, the company said that the rumors of a major discovery were overly optimistic. Four days later it confirmed the discovery of one of the richest strikes ever made in North America. In response, the SEC filed a civil lawsuit against the company and thirteen of its officers for violations of Section 10(b) and Rule 10b-5 of the 1934 act.

The SEC alleged that the press release was false and misleading because it failed to disclose the material fact of the discovery of a mine. It was also not timely because the company waited until April to release information that its directors had known since March. The Texas Gulf officers, on the other hand, contended (a) that the release was issued with good intentions to stop the rumors about a major discovery before they played havoc with the company's stock price and (b) that until the final test was completed on the day before they finally announced the find, they were not sure they had a major discovery. The Court of Appeals agreed with the SEC, finding that the company and its representatives were liable for issuing a materially misleading press release regardless of the motive behind the release or whether anyone profited from it.

The courts and the SEC have made it clear that public relations agencies cannot escape liability for misleading investors
simply by saying they were relying on their corporate client's
representations. A public relations agency must undertake a
"reasonable investigation" to satisfy itself that the representations are accurate.[44]

Selective Disclosure

In 2000, concerned that some companies were selectively
disclosing nonpublic material information to securities professionals who might later trade stocks on the basis of that information, the SEC adopted Regulation FD (Fair Disclosure).[45] Under
Regulation FD, a company must publicly disclose any material
information simultaneously with its disclosure to a securities
professional. If, however, a company unintentionally discloses
nonpublic material information to a securities professional, then
it must make the same disclosure to the public within twenty-
four hours of learning of the unintentional disclosure. A company can make the information public either by filing a form with
the SEC or by a method that will "effect broad, non-exclusionary
distribution of the information to the public."[46] Usually disclosure will be made by distributing a news release through a news
wire service.

The selective disclosure rule does not apply to information
provided to a person who owes the company a duty of trust or
confidence or who agrees to keep the information in confidence.
A public relations agency hired by a company, then, could receive
nonpublic material information without violating Rule 100 of
Regulation FD provided no one traded on the information.

The need for such a regulation arises in part because of the
increased ability of companies to communicate directly with
investors via the Internet. At one time, companies relied on securities analysts to serve as information intermediaries between
companies and investors. Investors, in turn, relied on analysts
for advice on a company's value as an investment. The ability of
investors to research companies via the Internet has reduced the
importance of analysts for some investors.

Not all investors have access to the Internet, however, or the
inclination to use the Internet. As a result, the SEC requires that
companies send material information to traditional media outlets prior to posting that information to the Internet. As a result,
distribution services such as Business Wire and PR Newswire

send releases on behalf of their client companies to all news wire services such as Associated Press and Reuters fifteen minutes before they post the releases to their Web sites. The time lag is to ensure a level playing field for investors.

Insider Trading

Selective disclosure is akin to insider trading—the buying or selling of shares by an insider—which has long been prohibited by the SEC. The rule against insider trading is to prevent the "privileged few [from gaining] an informational edge—and the ability to use that edge to profit—from their superior access to corporate insiders, rather than from their skill, acumen, or diligence."[47] An insider possesses material information that is unavailable to the general public. An insider who fails to wait for the information to become public before trading on the basis of the information will be liable under Rule 10b-5. Insiders, for the purposes of Rule 10b-5, include directors, officers, employees, and agents of the company, as well as those who have acquired such information through their positions, such as accountants, lawyers, consultants, and public relations professionals.

Insider trading became a prominent issue in 2003 when the SEC sued Martha Stewart civilly for engaging in illegal insider trading.[48] The suit alleged that Stewart had sold stock in ImClone Systems, Inc., a biopharmaceutical firm, on December 27, 2001, after receiving material nonpublic information from her broker to the effect that the ImClone CEO and his daughter had just sold their stock in the company. That information was material because the company was awaiting a decision from the FDA on whether it could market an experimental cancer drug. The selling of the CEO's stock suggested that the FDA decision was going to be negative. On August 7, 2006, the SEC and Stewart reached a settlement in which she agreed to pay a total of $195,081 (representing the losses she avoided by selling plus a civil penalty) and to a five-year ban on serving as a director of a public company.[49]

Rule 10b-5, as noted by the appeals court in *SEC v. Texas Gulf Sulphur*, also applies "to one possessing the information who may not be strictly termed an 'insider' within the meaning of [the act]" but who "tips off" financial consultants or confidantes about the nonpublic material information.[50] Public relations professionals are often in receipt of such information in the course of their dealings with corporations and must take care not to become "tippees" by revealing information to their friends and business partners.

At the heart of the ban on insider trading and tipping is the concept of fiduciary duty, which is a part of a corporation's duty to its shareholders to act at all times in the best interests of the corporation. Using nonpublic information to trade in the corporation's securities without first disclosing that information may well constitute a breach of that fiduciary duty and subject the corporation and its officers to lawsuits by the SEC and individual investors. Texas Gulf Sulphur and its management, for example, faced more than 100 civil suits filed by investors, claiming damages totaling $390 million.[51]

Sarbanes–Oxley Act

In October 2001, the energy company Enron announced that the SEC was investigating it for certain financial improprieties. The bad news for corporate America did not end there. Worldcom, Tyco, Global Crossing, Arthur Andersen, HealthSouth, and Martha Stewart became household names over the next few months, not for their ability to generate a profit, but for their unethical and sometimes illegal business practices. In response, Congress quickly enacted the Sarbanes–Oxley Act, which President Bush signed into law on July 30, 2002.[52] The purpose of the act is to make CEOs more responsible for the actions of their corporation and to make corporate and accounting fraud harder to get away with.

Like Regulation FD, the Act seeks to make corporate finances more transparent, requiring that companies file, "on a rapid and current basis" and in plain English, material changes in the company's financial condition or operations. No longer can companies keep material information about their financial condition private so long as insiders do not trade on the information, as was the situation after the *Texas Gulf Sulphur* case. Now companies must disclose such information to the public regardless of insider intent. The effect of the Sarbanes–Oxley Act is to make public corporations more accountable to their shareholders.

SEC Remedies

The SEC has the power to seek civil injunctions, to recommend criminal prosecutions, and to issue orders censuring, suspending, or expelling broker-dealers, investment advisors, and investment companies. It also may impose administrative penalties of up to $500,000. In addition to the federal laws, each state has its own laws regulating the sales of securities within its borders. Commonly called "blue sky laws," these statutes all have provisions prohibiting fraud in the sale of securities.

Other Federal Regulations Affecting Promotional Activities

Labor Relations

The Labor Management Relations Act of 1947 (Taft–Hartley Act) provides that management may communicate with its employees about political issues and labor relations provided it does so in a nonthreatening manner.[53] For example, management cannot threaten to fire or punish employees if they side with a union. The Taft–Hartley Act also ensures that management bargains with unions in good faith. Management cannot seek to undermine a union's position and influence by communicating directly with the employees about labor issues during collective bargaining negotiations. Because public relations practitioners are often involved with employee relations, it is imperative that they understand labor laws so that they do not violate those laws, especially during the collective bargaining process.

Lotteries

Lotteries, except for those permitted by statute and run by a governmental agency, are banned in all states. A lottery has three elements:

- a prize, which may be money, a trip, merchandise, etc.;
- chance, which means that luck, not skill, determines the winner; and
- consideration, which is the expense or effort required of the participant, such as the buying of a ticket or the entering in a draw.

All three elements must be present to constitute a lottery. Advertising of lotteries was prohibited until the Charity Games Advertising Clarification Act of 1988 relaxed the ban.[54] The amendment allows publishers and broadcasters in states where lotteries are legal to advertise in those states. Lotteries still cannot be advertised in states where they are illegal.[55]

Contests and Other Promotions

Contests contain any two of the three elements of a lottery. Most contests avoid the ban on lotteries by basing winning on a skill-testing question, as opposed to luck or chance, or including the statement "No purchase necessary" to avoid the consideration element. Although a public relations professional should check with the relevant state laws governing contests and promotions before engaging in any such activity, at a minimum, promotional materials for contests should include:

• eligibility requirements of being a contestant;

• rules and conditions for entering;

• true chances of winning; and

• description, value, and number of prizes.

For various reasons, an organization often will want to publicize the name and photograph of the contest winner in the local media after the event. If the organization intends to do so, consent to such publication should be made a condition of entering and explicitly stated in the promotional materials. The organization has no right to use the person's name and photograph without consent. Obtaining consent after the contest is much harder than making it part of the contest rules.

Money

In 1984, the Supreme Court upheld a federal statute regulating the representation of American currency, finding that the government has a substantial interest in preventing counterfeiting.[56] Money must be pictured only in black and white and either less than three-fourths or more than one and one-half times its actual size.

Summary

Public relations professionals who engage in lobbying for their clients must register with the government, either federal or state. They must also be aware of the various governmental regulations and agencies that affect their clients. The most common agencies that public relations professionals deal with are the FTC, the FDA, and the SEC. Each has its own rules and requirements, which must be obeyed. Regulations affecting contests and promotions must also be considered before the materials are prepared.

Discussion Questions

1. In its May 2000 report to the SEC and shareholders, Microsoft did not disclose that the government was seeking to divide up the company. Microsoft contended that it was not a material fact and did not need to be disclosed because the company would be vindicated on appeal. Was Microsoft legally correct in deciding that the information was not material? Was it ethically correct? How might you have advised Microsoft to handle the information?

2. What is the purpose of requiring lobbyists to register with the government? Is registration the most effective way of achieving that purpose?

3. Pharmaceutical companies have been lobbying the FDA to reduce the restrictions on advertising prescription drugs. The companies are arguing that the rules on commercial speech should be more lax. What are the arguments on both sides of the issue?

Notes

[1] Lobbying Disclosure Act, 2 U.S.C.S. §1601 *et seq.* (2002).

[2] "Lawmakers Enact Lobbying Reforms," *Congressional Quarterly 1995 Almanac: 104th Congress* (Washington, DC: Congressional Quarterly, 1996), sec. 1, 40.

[3] Ibid.

[4] 22 U.S.C. §611 *et seq.* (1988). See original act at 52 *U.S. Statutes at Large*, pp. 631–633, or PL 583, 8 June 1938.

[5] 22 U.S.C. §611(b) (2002).

[6] Ronald Moore, R. Farrar, and Erik Collins, *Advertising and Public Relations Law* (Mahwah, NJ: Erlbaum, 1998).

[7] Federal Trade Commission Act, 15 U.S.C.A. sec. 45(n)(West Supp. 1995).

[8] Ken Middleton, B. Chamberlin, and Matthew Bunker, *The Law of Public Communication*, 4th ed. (New York: Longman, 1997).

[9] *In re Cliffdale Assocs., Inc.*, 103 FTC 110 (1984).

[10] *FTC v. Colgate-Palmolive Co.*, 380 U.S. 374 (1965).

[11] *Warner-Lambert Co. v. FTC*, 562 F. 2d 749 (D.C. Cir. 1977), *cert. denied*, 435 U.S. 950 (1988).

[12] *FTC v. Peoples Credit First*, 2005 U.S. Dist. LEXIS 38545' 2006-1 Trade Cas. (CCH) P75,192.

[13] *In re Cliffdale*, 103 FTC (1984).

[14] *In re Pfizer, Inc.*, 81 FTC 23 (1972).

[15] *In re Thompson Medical Co.*, 104 FTC 648 (1984).

[16] "FTC Takes Action Against Marketers of Top-Selling Xenadrine EFX," http://www.ftc.gov/opa/2005/07/xenadrine.htm (accessed February 22, 2007).

[17] Federal Trade Commission Press Advisory, No. C-3582 (June 7, 1995).

[18] *In re General Foods Corp.*, 84 FTC 1572 (1974).

[19] ITT Continental Baking Co., 3 Trade Reg. Rptr. 20, 464 (1973).

[20] W. Washburn, "FTC Regulation of Endorsements in Advertising: In Consumer's Behalf?" *Pepperdine Law Review* 8 (1981): 697–745.

[21] "FTC Takes Action."

[22] Guides Concerning Use of Endorsements and Testimonials in Advertising, 16 C.F.R. §255.4 (1995).

[23] *In re Cooga Mooga*, 92 F.T.C. 310 (1978).

[24] Middleton, Chamberlin, and Bunker, *The Law of Public Communication*.

[25] Enforcement Policy Statement on Food Advertising, 59 Fed. Reg. 28,388 (1994).

[26] "FTC Takes Action."

[27] *In re ITT Continental Baking Co.*, 79 F.T.C. 248 (1971).

[28] Quoted in Donald Pember, *Mass Media Law* (Madison, WI: Brown & Benchmark, 1996), 500.

[29] P. Heald, "Money Damages and Corrective Advertising: An Economic Analysis," *University of Chicago Law Review* 55 (1988): 629–658.

[30] "Herbal-Cigarette Makers Settle Charges by FTC," *Wall Street Journal*, April 28, 2000, B6.

[31] Moore, Farrar, and Collins, *Advertising and Public Relations Law*.

[32] Food, Drug and Cosmetic Act, § 353(b)(1)(g).

[33] Moore, Farrar, and Collins, *Advertising and Public Relations Law*.

[34] *United States v. Articles of Drugs*, 392 F. 2d 21 (1967); *United States v. Guardian Chemical*, 410 F. 2d 157 (1969).

[35] "Improper DTC Ads Targeted Patients 'Worried' About Strokes," *Drug Industry Daily*, August 11, 2003, no. 156.

[36] "BMS Begins Correcting Misleading Pravachol Ads," *Drug Industry Daily*, February 24, 2004, no. 37.

[37] *FDA v. Brown & Williamson*, No. 98–1152 (2000).

[38] http://www.sec.gov.

[39] 15 U.S.C. sec. 77a *et seq.* (1988).

[40] *SEC v. Arvida Corporation*, 169 F. Supp. 211 (1958).

[41] *In re Carl M. Loeb, Rhoades & Co.*, 38 SEC 843, 853 (1959).

[42] 15 U.S.C. sec. 78a *et seq.* (1988).

[43] *SEC v. Texas Gulf Sulphur*, 401 F. 2d 833 (1968), *cert. denied*, 394 U.S. 976 (1969).

[44] *SEC v. Pig 'N' Whistle Corp.*, [1971–1972 Transfer Binder] Fed. Sec. L. Rep. (CCH) para. 93,384 (N.D. Ill. 1972); *In re Howard Bronson & Co.*, SEC Release No. 21138 (July 12, 1984).

[45] Selective Disclosure and Insider Trading, 17 C.F.R. Pts. 240, 243, 249.

[46] Ibid.

[47] Ibid.

[48] *SEC v. Stewart and Bacanovic*, 03 Civ. 4070 (S.D.N.Y.), http://www.sec.gov/litigation/complaints/comp18169.htm (accessed April 19, 2007).

[49] "Martha Stewart and Peter Bacanovic Agree to Settle SEC Insider Trading Charges," SEC Litigation Release No. 19794, August 7, 2006, http://www.sec.gov/litigation/litreleases/2006/lr19794.htm.

[50] *SEC v. Texas Gulf Sulphur*, 401 F. 2d, at 848.

[51] Moore, Farrar, and Collins, *Advertising and Public Relations Law*.

[52] Sarbanes–Oxley Act, 116 Stat. 745.

[53] 29 U.S.C. §158(c) (1988).

[54] 18 U.S.C.S. §1301 (2002).

[55] *United States v. Edge Broadcasting Co.*, 113 S. Ct. 2696 (1993).

[56] *Regan v. Time, Inc.* 468 U.S. 641 (1984).

chapter four

HARMING OTHERS

A tort is a civil wrong or injury committed by a person against another person or the property of another person. Torts involve civil law rather than criminal law. Criminal law involves crimes against society, and defendants are prosecuted by district attorneys. Defendants are found either innocent or guilty. If guilty, defendants face potential fines, sentences, or probation. Civil laws are injuries against individuals and are pursued by those individuals. The plaintiff (the person wronged) brings a lawsuit against the defendant (the person who committed the wrong). Defendants are found either liable or not liable for the plaintiff's injuries. If found liable, defendants in civil actions face judgments for damages, which usually is monetary compensation awarded to make up for the wrong suffered.

The law of torts is a product of common law. Common law is the set of legal principles and rules that have developed through judicial decisions as opposed to through statutes and legislative enactments. In the United States, each state has its own common law; there is no federal common law. Much of the common law of torts has been codified in state statutes. Because the law of torts varies from state to state, public relations professionals are wise to become familiar with the laws of the state in which they are employed. The most common torts public relations professionals need to be aware of are libel, invasion of privacy, negligence, and product liability.

Damaging Another's Reputation

Laws against libel, or defamation as it is also known, recognize the importance of reputation to an individual's integrity and seeks to protect individuals from false statements made by others. A defamatory statement is one that holds a person up to public hatred, ridicule, or scorn.[1] Individuals can be injured by a defamatory statement in three ways:

1. Their reputation can be damaged because the statement lowers them in the eyes of others, making others think less of them.

2. They can be deprived of the right to enjoy social contacts because people shun them.

3. Their ability to work or hold a job can be impaired.

Journalists need to understand defamation, or libel law, so that they can be as aggressive as possible in pursuing stories, especially those that involve government officials. Public relations professionals, however, need to understand libel so that they do not unnecessarily harm their publics. They also need to be aware of the law so that they can spot potentially defamatory statements about their organization made by others. Although the final decision as to whether a statement is defamatory and actionable would never be theirs, they are the first line of defense against such statements because they are constantly scanning their environment for mentions of their clients.

Defamation can take the form of libel or slander. Libel is the term used to describe written defamatory statements, while slander is used for oral defamatory statements. Traditionally, the courts treated libel more seriously because it was believed that the written word had more permanence. Writing also involves more thought. Spoken words, on the other hand, are often spontaneous and reach fewer people. Things can be said in a moment of anger, but the moment passes, and so do the words. As a result, with slander, the plaintiff has to prove that an actual financial loss occurred because of the statement.

Television and radio broadcasts have blurred the distinctions between libel and slander because they reach a wide audience and often come from a prepared script. As a result, many states consider defamatory statements made during television or radio broadcasts to be libel, not slander. But if the statements made during a broadcast are spontaneous and not scripted, an action for slander may ensue. The actor Carroll O'Connor, for example, was sued for slander because of comments he made about his son's drug supplier after his son's suicide in 1995.[2] In an interview on national television, O'Connor called the man "a partner in murder." The jury found in favor of O'Connor. Because "libel" is the more commonly used term, it will be used here.

Who Can Sue?

A plaintiff can not only be an individual, but also a corporate or organizational entity that participates in the public sphere. The following is a brief list of those who can or cannot bring a suit to court.

- **Individuals.** Every individual may sue for libel. But because libel is a personal action based on damage to an individual's reputation, it expires with the death of the individual. The dead cannot be libeled, because they cannot suffer injuries. In some states, however, family members may continue an action if the plaintiff dies during litigation. At common law, relatives of the dead cannot institute a suit for damages to the reputation of the deceased family member.

- **Corporations.** A for-profit corporation must show it suffered a loss in sales as a result of the defamatory statement; a not-for-profit corporation must show it lost public support and contributions.

- **Unincorporated Associations, Organizations, and Societies.** States vary in allowing unincorporated groups, such as labor unions, political action committees, and trade associations, to sue in their own right.

- **Governments.** Governments at any level—federal, state, county, municipal—and government agencies cannot sue for libel. For example, a local school board could not sue if someone claimed it engaged in discriminatory practices. But the individual members of the school board could sue if they were sufficiently identified and suffered damage.

The Plaintiff's Burden of Proof

The plaintiff in a libel action must prove all six essential elements to win a libel case:

1. Publication
2. Identification
3. Defamation
4. Fault

5. Falsity

6. Injury

Publication

Publication, for the purposes of libel, means that at least one person in addition to the writer and the defamed person saw or heard the material. If Stan sends an e-mail to his friend, Linda, in which he defames his boss, Stella, he has published the libel and can be sued by Stella. If Linda, in turn, were to forward the message on to her friend Jim, she has republished the libel and could also be sued by Stella. Every republication of the libel constitutes a new libel.

Publishers of newspapers, magazines, trade publications, and even newsletters are considered responsible for everything they publish and, therefore, are subject to actions for libel, regardless of whether they wrote the material. Liability is based on the understanding that publishers, or at least their employees, determine what goes into their publications. In contrast, common carriers, such as telephone companies, are not responsible for the information transmitted via their service. Common carriers exercise no control over content and therefore are not responsible for it. In between the two are distributors. Distributors, such as bookstores and libraries, are not expected to have knowledge about everything found on their shelves. They are not considered responsible for content unless they know or should have known of the defamatory statement. Under what are known as the "Good Samaritan" provisions of the Communications Decency Act of 1996, Internet service providers and users of interactive computer services are not considered publishers even if they restrict "objectionable" messages on their services.[3] The Communications Decency Act also protects Web sites that publish defamatory information that was written by a third party. Plaintiffs can only seek damages from the original source of the information.

Identification

The plaintiff must show that the statement was "of and concerning him, her, or it."[4] Many libel actions arise as a result of the misnaming of individuals. For example, in 1982, Ben Nesbitt sued the *Asheville (NC) Citizen* over a story that accused him of being charged with larceny. It was actually his son, Ben Eugene Nesbitt, who had been arrested and charged.[5] It is to avoid such lawsuits that journalists identify individuals as fully as possible using age, address, and full name.

A plaintiff can be defamed, however, without being explicitly named. A newspaper columnist lost a libel suit based on an item reporting gossip in Palm Beach of an affair between the wife of a wealthy pillar of society and a former FBI agent who had become an attorney.[6] No names were mentioned in the column, but at the time there was only one attorney in Palm Beach who had been an FBI agent and who socialized with the wealthy. The court held that the attorney had been sufficiently identified in the column. If even one person in the community would recognize the person libeled, then there has been sufficient identification.

Sometimes members of a group are libeled. The rule of thumb for group identification is that if the group has fewer than fifteen members, then each member of the group probably has been identified. If the group has more than 100 members, there is no identification. For groups falling in the middle, there may be identification if a blanket slur is used. For example, the Oklahoma Supreme Court, in upholding a jury award to a University of Oklahoma football player who had sued for defamation, said that all sixty members of the University of Oklahoma football team had been libeled in a 1985 article in *True* magazine. The article said that team members used an amphetamine nasal spray to make them more aggressive.[7] Using the adjective "most" or "many" turns the allegation into a partial slur and makes identification less likely. Had the article about the Oklahoma football team said that most members or many members used the nasal spray, no individual player could argue he had been identified by the article.

Defamation

Defamation is holding someone up to public hatred, ridicule, or scorn. It is more than just saying something that is embarrassing or private about a person. It is saying something negative about a person's character that causes others to think less of that person. A statement can either be libelous on its face (libel per se) or libelous when other facts are known (libel per quod). Allegations of criminal conduct, incompetence, and sexual impropriety are examples of libel per se. Calling someone a communist or a homosexual has been considered defamatory and libel per se. And alleging that someone suffers from a "loathsome disease" can be libelous.[8]

In regard to professionals and businesspeople, to suggest a pattern of incompetence or shoddy workmanship is considered defamatory; any statement alluding to these qualities should be made carefully. Comparison ads are not generally a problem provided the ad does not suggest that the competitor deceives the consumer or engages in unethical behavior.

With libel per quod, the statement appears innocent on its face but becomes defamatory when added to information the reader or viewer already knows. For example, an article that falsely says a woman has had a baby is libelous if the woman can prove that readers would know she is single.[9] In addition, she must prove special damages; that is, she must prove she suffered actual monetary loss as a result of the defamation.

Fault

Under the common law prior to 1964, once the plaintiff proved publication, identification, and defamation, the court presumed that the plaintiff had suffered harm from the statements. It did not matter whether the defendant intended to cause harm; the question was simply whether a defamatory statement had been made. But in *New York Times v. Sullivan* in 1964, the Supreme Court held that the plaintiff, if a public official, also had to show that the defendant was at fault in publishing the defamatory statement.[10] In 1974, the Supreme Court established four categories of plaintiffs to be used in determining the level of fault required:

1. Public official
2. All-purpose public figure
3. Limited purpose public figure
4. Private person

Public Official.   *New York Times v. Sullivan* involved a full-page ad run on March 29, 1960, in the *New York Times* by a committee of civil rights activists. Titled "Heed Their Rising Voices," the ad sought support for students at Alabama State College who were engaged in nonviolent demonstrations. The ad accused the Montgomery, Alabama, police of meeting the students' efforts with "an unprecedented wave of terror." Montgomery Police Commissioner L. B. Sullivan sued the *New York Times* for libel, arguing that the allegations against the police reflected on him personally. A trial court awarded Sullivan $500,000 in damages, which was upheld on appeal by the Alabama Supreme Court.

The U.S. Supreme Court found that Sullivan had been criticized for the manner in which he had conducted his official business, the very kind of speech that the First Amendment was designed to protect. The United States is committed on a national level to robust, open debate, the Court declared, and with such debate, erroneous statements are inevitably going to be made. Sullivan had voluntarily assumed a position in government in which he had to expect to receive some criticism and complaint. Public officials need to have thick skins. They also have access to the media to refute any defamatory statements made about them. They have at their disposal the means to rebut the criticism and to rebuild their reputation if harmed.

As a result, the Court held, public officials have to prove that the defendant published the statement with actual malice—knowledge of falsity or reckless disregard of the truth. Actual malice does not mean ill will or spite. It means that the defendant knew the statement was false or that he or she recklessly disregarded the truth and published it anyway. In cases since *Sullivan*, the Supreme Court has said plaintiffs can establish reckless disregard if they can prove the defamatory statements were made with a "high degree of awareness of their probable falsity" or "if the defendant in fact entertained serious doubts as to the truth of his publication."[11]

In deciding whether the statement was published with actual malice, the courts look at such factors as:

- Did the information come from reliable sources?

- Is the information probable? In other words, was the information so unlikely that it cried out for further examination?

- Were some known facts omitted that would have established the falsity of the statement?

- Were warnings that the information was false ignored?

- Were inconsistencies in the information disregarded?[12]

It is safe to say that any person elected to government office is a public official for the purposes of libel law. In addition, a wide range of other government employees qualify as public officials. The term includes those who have, or appear to the public to have, substantial responsibility for or control over the conduct of government affairs. A public official for the purposes of libel holds a position that invites public scrutiny. Often the position is one that involves policy-making decisions.

Examples of plaintiffs courts have held to be public officials are federal and state legislators, mayors, town council members, school board members, elected judges, police officers, university presidents, and administrators who spend taxpayers' money. Even a research analyst for the Senate Energy and Utilities Commission was deemed a public official because she was the top expert in nuclear waste management and the major source of information to senators.[13] A research director at a public mental health hospital and public schoolteachers have been held not to be public officials for the purposes of libel.[14]

A person who works for the government in a position of authority will be deemed a public official for the purposes of a lawsuit if the defamatory statement pertains to either the manner in which the plaintiff conducts official business or the plaintiff's fitness to hold office. Generally, the lower persons are on the scale of public officialdom, the more the law will protect their private lives. Because of the immense responsibilities of the position, almost everything the president of the United States does reflects upon his fitness to hold office. The private life of a U.S. senator is probably open to less scrutiny than the private life of the president, but more investigation into the senator's life will be permitted than into the life of a city police officer.

It is difficult for a plaintiff to prove actual malice because it requires proving that the defendant knew the statement was false or recklessly disregarded the truth. In setting the standard in *New York Times v. Sullivan*, the Supreme Court made it difficult for public officials to win libel suits because it wanted to encourage open discussion of their actions.

In the years following *New York Times v. Sullivan*, the Supreme Court had the opportunity to examine the issue of libel on several occasions and began to expand its public official category to a general one of public figure. In *Gertz v. Welch* (1974), the Court considered the issue of categorizing plaintiffs and their level of burden of proof. Elmer Gertz, a prominent lawyer, represented the family of a boy who had been killed by a Chicago police officer. *American Opinion* magazine, published by the right-wing John Birch Society, accused Gertz of being part of a nationwide conspiracy to discredit law enforcement agencies. The magazine called him a Leninist and a communist-fronter. Gertz brought suit against the magazine. At trial, the issue was whether the plaintiff, who had been involved in a high-profile case, had to prove actual malice. That is, should he be considered a public figure for the purposes of a libel action? The Supreme Court decided that Gertz did not have to prove actual malice, that he was in fact just somebody doing his job, a job that happened to draw media attention.[15] In so deciding, the Court outlined two kinds of public figures: all-purpose and limited purpose.

All-Purpose Public Figures.   All-purpose public figures are individuals who have assumed roles of special prominence in the affairs of society. They have pervasive power and influence and have achieved widespread fame and notoriety to the point that their names are household words. These individuals have ready access to the media and can easily refute any allegations against them. As a result, all-purpose public figures, like public officials, have to prove actual malice. Long-time host of the *Tonight Show* Johnny Carson, political writer William F. Buckley, Jr., and a publicly owned insurance company with assets of a billion dollars have been held to be all-purpose public figures.[16]

Limited Purpose Public Figures.   The second group outlined by the Court in *Gertz* were individuals who voluntarily thrust themselves into the vortex of a public controversy to affect the outcome. These individuals are public figures only for defamatory statements related to the controversy in question. That is why they are limited purpose public figures. If the libel is related to the public controversy, they have to prove actual malice.

The courts first look to determine whether there is a public controversy, which has been defined by the courts as a real debate, the outcome of which affects a segment of the general public. An award-winning high school football player was ruled not to be a limited purpose public figure because he was not part of a controversy. "The mere fact of playing on a high school football team, or little league baseball team, or a college golf team, is not in and of itself a controversy," the court held.[17] Once the courts conclude there is a controversy, they examine the plaintiff's role in that controversy. The most important aspect is the voluntary nature of the role. Individuals have to take positive steps to thrust themselves into the center of the controversy and subsequent media attention. Individuals who are charged with an infamous crime are not automatically limited public figures because they have not voluntarily thrust themselves into the media glare.[18] Nor does receiving public funds automatically make a plaintiff a limited purpose public figure.[19] And finally, the courts look to see whether the defamation arose out of the plaintiff's participation in the controversy. Therefore, the scope of the controversy defines the scope of the public personality.

The case of *Bieter* v. *Fetzer* illustrates the process used by the courts.[20] The case arose after the 2002 death of U.S. Senator Paul Wellstone in an airplane crash. There was no immediate explanation for the crash of the small plane, but because the crash occurred about a week before an election (in which Wellstone was involved in a tight race for his senatorial seat), conspiracy theories abounded. One of the conspiracy theorists was James Fetzer, a university professor. Fetzer published articles in an alternative newspaper in which he suggested that high-ranking Republicans in the George W. Bush administration were behind Wellstone's death. Bieter, a former prosecutor and Republican, started an Internet chat group to refute Fetzer's claims. In response, Fetzer alleged in the chat room that Bieter had been deprived of his right to practice law and had been charged with sexual harassment. Bieter sued Fetzer for defamation. The court of appeals found that the conspiracy debate was a real controversy and that by forming the chat room to discuss and refute Fetzer's claims, and by holding himself up as an authority in the debate, Bieter became a limited purpose public figure. The defamatory statements to the effect that Bieter had been deprived of his ability to practice law were related to the controversy because they called into question his credibility as an expert.

Individuals who voluntarily try to change the mind of others about public issues are often considered limited purpose public figures. For example, an outspoken opponent of fluoridating water, a circulator of a petition, and Liberty Lobby, a citizens' lobby group, have been held to be limited purpose public figures.[21]

Usually corporations will not be considered public figures unless they go beyond ordinary advertising and public relations practices.[22] Companies engaging in aggressive advertising and public relations campaigns regarding a controversial issue, or organizations previously involved in a public dispute, may, however, find themselves to be public figures in a libel action.[23] A company that promotes itself as proactive in environmental matters, for example, could be considered a public figure in matters involving the environment.

The courts require public figures, all-purpose and limited purpose, to prove actual malice because they seek their status by playing an influential role in the affairs of society and thereby voluntarily expose themselves to an increased risk of public scrutiny. Also, public figures have access to channels of effective communication so that they can counter false statements about them. Private persons, on the other hand, are more vulnerable to injury.

Private Persons.   Plaintiffs who do not fit into any of the three categories discussed above are private persons. In *Gertz*, the Supreme Court left it up to the states to determine the level of fault private persons have to prove in a libel action, provided some level of fault is required. States have the option of choosing among three possible levels of fault: actual malice, gross negligence or gross irresponsibility, and negligence. Actual malice is the same as for public officials and public figures. It involves proving knowledge of falsity or reckless disregard for the truth. Negligence is the failure to exercise the standard of care that a reasonable person would exercise in similar circumstances. Gross negligence falls between the two. The majority of states have chosen negligence as the level of fault private person plaintiffs need to prove in libel actions, but at least one state, New York, has chosen gross irresponsibility.[24]

Falsity

Prior to 1964 and *New York Times v. Sullivan*, once the plaintiff proved publication, identification, and defamation, the falsity of the statement was presumed. That is why truth was a defense in such cases. Because public officials, all-purpose public figures, and limited purpose public figures have to prove actual malice— knowledge of falsity or reckless disregard of the truth—they also have to prove that the statement was in fact false.

The issue is more complicated for private persons. The *Gertz* Court did not say that private persons had to prove falsity, only fault. In 1986, however, the Court held that private persons involved in matters of public concern also had to bear the burden of proving that the statement was false. In *Philadelphia v. Hepps*, a corporation that owned a chain of Thrifty stores sued the *Philadelphia Inquirer* for linking the chain to organized crime.[25] The *Inquirer* said the Thrifty chain, which sold beer, soft drinks, and snacks, used its criminal connections to obtain favorable rulings from the state liquor control board. Pennsylvania law required private plaintiffs to prove negligence in libel actions but not that the statements were false.

The Supreme Court held that private plaintiffs involved in matters of public concern also had to prove falsity. The Court reasoned that public officials and public figures are required to show falsity as part of actual malice and that the First Amendment protects speech about public figures and matters of public concern.

To ensure that truthful speech was not deterred, private plaintiffs involved in matters of public concern also had to prove falsity.

The Court has never defined public concern, but presumably if the media are publishing the information or if a business is putting out a news release about it, then the matter is of public concern. Private persons not involved in matters of public concern do not have to prove falsity.

Injury

Three kinds of damages can be awarded in civil lawsuits: general, special, and punitive.

General. If public officials, all-purpose public figures, and limited purpose public figures are able to prove actual malice on the part of the defendant, the court presumes that the defamatory statements injured them. These plaintiffs are then awarded general damages, which is a sum of money to compensate them for their presumed loss of reputation and injury to their good name. It also is meant to compensate them for their presumed pain and suffering.

In *Dun & Bradstreet v. Greenmoss Builders,* the U.S. Supreme Court held that presumed damages also applied to private persons not involved in matters of public concern who could prove negligence on the part of the defendant.[26] A new employee of Dun & Bradstreet, a business financial and credit reporting service, wrote in a report that Greenmoss Builders had filed for bankruptcy. It was actually one of Greenmoss's employees who had filed for bankruptcy, not the company itself. Greenmoss sued Dun & Bradstreet for libel, arguing that the credit report damaged its reputation. The Supreme Court held that Greenmoss's credit rating was a private matter, of interest only to Greenmoss and the people who did business with it. Greenmoss was therefore presumed to have suffered damages by virtue of the libelous comments that were made about it.

Private persons who are involved in matters of public concern, after proving the defendant was negligent, must also prove they were injured. They have to prove they suffered actual harm, such as loss of reputation, personal humiliation, or mental anguish.

When determining general damage awards, whether presumed or actual, juries consider the degree of fault, the number of people who may have read or heard the defamation, the seriousness of the defamatory charge, the degree of injury suffered, and the character and reputation of the plaintiff and defendant.

Special.   Special damages are out-of-pocket monetary losses suffered by the plaintiff. All plaintiffs have to prove these damages if they want to claim them. A therapist's or doctor's bill is an example of special damages. Essentially, they are expenses for which receipts can be provided.

Punitive.   Punitive damages are meant, just as they sound, to punish defendants for the libel. They have been described by the court as "private fines" levied by juries "to punish reprehensible conduct and to deter its future occurrence."[27] Before private plaintiffs involved in matters of public concern are entitled to punitive damages, they must prove actual malice.

Defenses to Libel Suits

At the end of the plaintiff's case, the defense offers its case. Defenses open to the defendant include:

- Statute of limitations
- Truth
- First Amendment opinion defense
- Privilege
- Consent

Statute of Limitations

Almost all criminal and civil actions or lawsuits are subject to a statute of limitations, meaning that an action must be commenced against the defendant within a certain time after the event. The time periods vary by state. Usually libel actions must be brought within one to two years from the date of publication, regardless of whether the plaintiff was aware of the libel at the time. The statute of limitations is an absolute defense. If the deadline is missed, no action for libel can be brought. For example, in a state with a one-year statute of limitations on libel, if a public relations department issued a news release on March 19 falsely indicating that an employee was terminated for embezzling funds, that employee would have until March 18 the following year to commence a lawsuit against the organization and the public relations practitioners for damages.

Truth

Traditionally, truth was the most important defense to libel actions. Now, because almost all plaintiffs have to prove falsity, truth has lost some of its importance as a defense. However, ensuring that the information is true prior to publication is still the best protection against libel actions. The information need only be substantially true, which means that the impact of the information would have been no different if the details had been accurate.

First Amendment Opinion Defense

Sometimes the plaintiff is unable to prove the falsity of a statement because it involves opinion and cannot be proved true or false. Describing someone as a "bad" accountant, for example, amounts to opinion. The Supreme Court in *Gertz v. Welch* established the First Amendment protection for statements of opinion when it said, "There is no such thing as a false idea."[28] Simply couching a statement of fact as an opinion is not sufficient, however. In other words, saying, "In my opinion, Jane Smith is an embezzler," does not make the statement an opinion.[29] It can still be proved false.

Two categories of statements are protected by the First Amendment opinion defense:

- vague evaluations incapable of being proved true or false; and
- statements that are exaggerated, including hyperbole, parody, and loose figurative language.

For example, according to the court of appeals, when Andy Rooney said on the television show *60 Minutes* that a product called Rain X did not work, he was not expressing a pure opinion but implying an objective fact.[30] Whether the product works is something that is subject to proof. But when *Hustler* magazine said that evangelist Jerry Falwell's "first time," implying his first sexual encounter, was with his mother in an outhouse, the Court said the statement was not subject to proof. It was parody, and something that no one would believe.[31] Similarly, statements made by a sales agent alleging that his former employer was anti-Semitic, had told anti-Semitic jokes, and had persecuted him for his Jewish heritage were considered statements of fact and not protected expressions of opinion. But statements that his former employer was sick, mentally ill, and living with two hundred cats were rhetorical hyperbole and therefore protected.[32]

Privilege

There are absolute privileges and qualified privileges. An absolute privilege protects the defendant regardless of motive or accuracy. A privilege in law means an exception to the normal rule. Government officials acting in their official capacity have absolute privilege from libel litigation. Statements made during the course of official proceedings are protected. A member of the House of Representatives can therefore say whatever he or she wants to on the floor of the House and not be sued for libel. All individuals taking part in judicial proceedings have an absolute privilege. Judges, attorneys, and witnesses cannot be sued for libelous statements made in open court.

A qualified privilege is an extension of the absolute privilege. Essentially, it permits others (e.g., journalists) to report libelous comments made in a privileged setting without in turn being held responsible for the statements. For a qualified privilege to apply, the defendant must establish that:

- It came from a privileged source.
- It was attributed to the source.
- The comment was fair and accurate.
- It was not motivated by common law malice.

Consent

If a person authorizes a story or article, he cannot later claim it was libelous. The public relations practice of having releases and articles approved prior to publication helps reduce the exposure of public relations practitioners to libel suits.

Disparagement

Defamation of a product, rather than the maker of the product, is called trade libel or trade disparagement. In trade libel, the product's quality or usefulness is defamed. For example, Boskovich Farms, a California farm, sued Taco Bell for trade libel in March 2007 after Taco Bell continued to link the farm's green onions to the December 2006 outbreak of E. coli that sickened more than 70 people in the Northeast even though the company knew the green onions were not the cause of the outbreak.[33] According to the lawsuit, Taco Bell officials knew by December 11 that the green onions were not the source of the disease, but Taco Bell president Greg Creed published an open letter in national newspapers two days later stating that "all Taco Bell ingredients have come back negative for E. coli . . . with the possible exception of green onions." Boskovich Farms claims to have lost "millions of dollars of business" as a result of Taco Bell's actions.

In disparagement lawsuits, the plaintiff must show that the defendant made the statement knowing it was false or with reckless disregard for its truth or falsity. Damages will be awarded for the monetary losses suffered directly as a result of the disparagement. Damages may also include expenses to counteract the false claims in the marketplace. Defenses to trade disparagement are the same as for libel.

Libel and Public Relations

Although the Supreme Court since 1964 has reduced the fear of libel actions for journalists with its actual malice standard, public relations professionals are wise to keep vigilant about potentially libelous statements in their materials. The Supreme Court's focus has always been on maintaining the ability of the public to criticize its government. There is less protection for individuals who might libel private persons in matters not of public concern, and such plaintiffs are more often the ones public relations professionals will run across. Internal memos explaining why an employee was fired, a negative reference letter, a newsletter article describing an employee in unflattering terms, or a press release that disparages a competitor's product may result in lawsuits. In each case, the individual defamed would most likely be a private person and the matter in question a private concern. The plaintiff would have to prove only that the defendant was negligent in publishing the libel.

One possible defense for businesses is a common law privilege for messages of mutual interest. At common law, companies have a qualified privilege to share information essential to the conduct of their business. Communications made during the ordinary course of business would be considered subject to a qualified privilege, provided they were made in good faith, bear a reasonable relation to the business purpose, and were made without malice.

An example of such a qualified privilege appears in the case of *Garziano v. E. I. DuPont de Nemours and Co.*[34] P. Richard Garziano was discharged after his supervisors concluded he had committed several acts of sexual harassment at work. When rumors about his firing circulated among the employees, the company issued a managers' information bulletin on sexual harassment. The bulletin referred to the "recent sexual harassment incident which resulted in an employee's termination." Garziano was not named in the bulletin, but his termination and reasons for it became the talk of the company and the community. Garziano sued DuPont for libel.

DuPont argued that the bulletin was protected by privilege. The company had a right to share accurate information about its actions and policies with its employees. On appeal, the court agreed that DuPont had the right to distribute the bulletin to its supervisors. The question nevertheless remained whether the privilege had been abused by the dissemination of the information about Garziano to individuals outside the plant. The court remanded the case to the trial judge to resolve that issue by looking at whether outside contractors were present at the DuPont plant at the time the bulletin was distributed and had access to the information. The *Garziano* case stands for the proposition that a business may be justified in providing its employees with defamatory information about an individual, but it is not justified in broadcasting that information beyond its employees.

Red Flags
Some words and expressions should raise red flags in the view of a public relations professional. Among them: addict, adultery, AIDS, alcoholic, bankrupt, blackmail, bribery, cheater, child abuse, corrupt, deadbeat, drug abuser, drunkard, ex-convict, fraud, hooker, incompetent, liar, mental disease, morally delinquent, perjurer, racist, scam, spy, unethical.

Strategies to Avoid Libel
Libel is a misrepresentation of truth. Therefore, always thoroughly research the material and present the information as accurately as possible. Sound basic journalism techniques such as checking sources and facts are the best defenses to libel actions. Other points to keep in mind:

- **Opinion.** Back up opinions with the facts that gave rise to them.

- **Quotations.** Be careful when editing quoted matter that the meaning is not changed, and make sure the quote accurately expresses the facts.

- **Identification.** Avoid innuendo and suggestive implication because the person may well still be identified. Identifying an employee in a newsletter only by his initials will not serve as a shield.

- **Clippings/news.** Be careful when relying on clippings or news articles if they defame someone. Either do not use the information or rephrase it.

- **Headlines/photos.** Do not hype a story with a title that inaccurately reflects the story's content. Do not include a photo of an individual or a small group to a story that could be defamatory. For example, do not include a photo of a random group with a news release on the spread of HIV in America.
- **Interviews/notes.** Retain all notes and tapes from interviews.
- **Edit.** Rewrite portions of a story that are libelous. Look at the story critically. Is there anything in it that could injure someone's reputation? If so, is it false? Edit any offending material.

When a Client Has Been Libeled

Although the final decision as to whether a statement made about a client is defamatory and actionable will be made by lawyers, in advising a client whether to seek legal assistance, public relations professionals should consider the:

- nature of the allegations;
- source of the defamatory statements;
- extent of the damage done to the client's reputation; and
- ability of the client to counter the statements in the mass media.

One problem with suing for libel is that the lawsuit itself may become newsworthy, which means the allegations will be repeated in the media, drawing more public attention than the initial statement did. Although a client may see a lawsuit as a means to defend its reputation, libel actions have a tendency to lend legitimacy to the statements. The danger of giving credibility to tabloids is one reason why Hollywood stars do not sue for libelous stories about them. Ignoring outrageous allegations is one way to get them to disappear.

A large corporation also needs to be careful that it does not lose in the court of public opinion by bringing a libel action. McDonald's, for example, won its libel suit against two activists but lost public sentiment because it appeared to be ganging up on the little guy. McDonald's would have been better advised to counter the allegations in its ads and through its actions.

Blogs, social networking sites, and message boards create other problems for public relations practitioners and their clients. First, the sheer number of these outlets makes it difficult for practitioners to monitor what is being said online about their clients. Second, the ease with which information can be shared and moved online from one site to another means that it is almost impossible to remove defamatory statements from the Internet entirely. And if they are not removed, they will remain somewhere online indefinitely. Third, it is difficult to find out the true identity of a poster for the purposes of a lawsuit. Subpoenaing the ISP for the user's identity has been used in the past, but Wi-Fi networks make even ISP's incapable of tracing the original user. The best public relations strategy is to have an online presence. That way, you will be prepared to respond effectively and quickly to address defamatory statements.[35]

Invading Another's Privacy

Privacy is either the right to be left alone or the right to control information about one's personal life. This idea of privacy was first clearly set out in an 1890 law review article by Samuel Warren and Louis Brandeis.[36] They said that an area of the law that protects an individual's privacy should be carved out. The old common law protected people from intrusion onto their property and to their person with trespassing, but it was privacy in a physical sense, an invasion of personal physical space. The notion of privacy advanced by Warren and Brandeis was more of a psychological privacy. They thought there should be some way to protect people from intrusive media.

In 1960, this idea of privacy was expanded and developed by legal scholar William Prosser.[37] He outlined and defined four torts of privacy:

- **Intrusion:** intruding on another's solitude.
- **Appropriation:** using someone's name or likeness without their consent to reap a profit.
- **False light:** painting a distorted picture in the mind of the public with a nondefamatory falsehood.
- **Public disclosure of embarrassing private facts:** publishing very private, personal information.

Intrusion

Intrusion is the offensive physical, electronic, or mechanical intrusion on another's solitude. It can involve trespassing, which is going onto someone's private property without their consent, or surveillance, which involves the use of equipment to enhance sight or hearing. Private homes have the greatest protection from intrusion; businesses have less protection. The determining factor is the expectation of privacy. Within their homes, people have a high expectation of privacy. They do not expect others to be listening to or watching them. In a public place, such as at a football game, people cannot expect much privacy. Others around them can overhear their conversations and see their actions.

The defense to intrusion is consent, explicit or implied. Explicit consent means that the property owner gave permission for others to be on the property. Implied consent is inferred but not stated. Stores give implied consent to the public to enter their premises to shop, but such consent can be exceeded. For example, in *Le Mistral v. CBS*, the court held that the restaurant Le Mistral had given its implied consent for people to come in and dine.[38] CBS, however, had exceeded that consent when it entered the restaurant with cameras rolling right at lunchtime to do a story on health problems.

Appropriation

Appropriation is the use of the name or likeness of someone without consent for commercial exploitation or purpose. The use of names in news stories is not considered commercial, even though the media are commercial enterprises. For appropriation to apply, the name or likeness must be used in an ad or a promotional piece. Private individuals sue for appropriation because they have been shamed or humiliated by the invasion of their privacy. Celebrities also sue for appropriation, but they are seeking the loss of the profit they could have gotten for the use of their name or likeness. Essentially, with celebrities it is a matter of controlling their right of publicity.

The first time the Supreme Court upheld the right of publicity was the 1977 case of *Zacchini v. Scripps Howard*.[39] Hugo Zacchini was the human cannonball. He shot himself out of a cannon at fairs. When he came into one town, a cameraman asked permission to film him for the evening news; Zacchini refused. The cameraman shot the footage anyway, and it aired that evening in a story about the fair. Zacchini's entire fifteen-second act was shown in the segment. Zacchini sued for appropriation, arguing that because his whole act had been shown, there was no reason for people to pay to see him. He argued that he should have control over his own publicity or should be compensated by others using his act. The Court agreed; Zacchini should be compensated for the use of the film. It might have been different had the station used only a portion of the act, but it used the whole thing, thereby stripping Zacchini of his livelihood. The Court defined the right of publicity as personal control over the commercial display and exploitation of one's personality and the exercise of one's talents.

The concept of name or likeness has been expanded over the years to include one's voice and persona. For example, former *Tonight Show* host Johnny Carson sued Here's Johnny Portable Toilets for using the expression "Here's Johnny" in its ads. Carson argued that "Here's Johnny" was so much a part of his persona that he should have control over its use, and the Sixth Circuit Court of Appeals agreed.[40] In another example, when singer Bette Midler refused to do a radio spot for a car dealership, the dealership hired one of Midler's backup singers who sounded exactly like Midler. The ad left the impression it was Midler singing. She sued for appropriation and won.[41]

Another development in the right of publicity area involves "life stories." The question is who owns the rights to a life story— the people involved or the journalist who writes a nonfiction account of the story? The issue arose from a Disney Corporation movie based on journalist Jonathan Harr's book, *A Civil Action*. The book is a nonfiction account of an outbreak of childhood leukemia and the ensuing legal battle in Massachusetts during the 1980s. Disney owned the movie rights to Harr's book, but the individuals involved argued that they owned the rights to their "life" story. Some states, Massachusetts among them, have attempted to restrict the use of such nonfiction works serving as the basis for movies without the consent of the people whose life story is the subject.

Defenses to appropriation are consent and newsworthiness. The newsworthy defense is not restricted to the news media. A "think tank" policy center was able to use the defense successfully when it was sued for appropriation because the publication in question concerned a matter of legitimate public concern.[42] The plaintiff sued the center for its use of a statement he made in its fund-raising letter. Specifically, the letter read, "By all measures the Mackinac Center has had an outstanding year and the people of Michigan are the beneficiaries. But you don't need to take my word for it. This fall Luigi Battaglieri . . . stated, 'Frankly, I admire what the Mackinac Center has done.'"[43] The plaintiff Battaglieri was generally a critic of the center's policies, which the letter went on to acknowledge, and thus claimed that the use of his name in the letter was a misappropriation of another's name for commercial benefit. The Michigan Court of Appeals found that although the letter clearly had a commercial purpose (to solicit funds), it contained information about public policy issues, which were matters of legitimate public concern.

Usually public relations professionals and photographers obtain consent from their subjects, which protects them from appropriation lawsuits unless the use exceeds the consent given.

False Light

False light is information that puts an individual into a false light that is highly offensive to a reasonable person. It is a non-defamatory, false statement. False light most often arises in fictionalized situations, as it did in the first invasion of privacy lawsuit heard by the Supreme Court.[44] James Hill, his wife, and five children were held hostage in their Philadelphia home by three escaped convicts. The Hills were not harmed in any way and later said the convicts treated them extremely well. A novel fictionalizing the account came out a year later and included some violence. That novel led to a Broadway play and a promotional review in *Life* magazine. Hill objected to a line in *Life*'s story that read the play was "a heart-stopping account of how a family rose to heroism in a crisis." Hill sued, claiming that the story put the family into a false light. They had tried to avoid publicity, and the story falsely portrayed them as heroes. The Supreme Court held that plaintiffs involved in matters of public concern must prove actual malice to win a false light action.

In *Battaglieri v. Mackinac Center for Public Policy*, Battaglieri also claimed that the letter put him in a false light because a reader could draw the inference that he was endorsing Mackinac's policies, not just expressing respect for its advocacy of those policies. The Michigan Court of Appeals held that such an inference was highly unlikely, especially since the letter specifically noted that Battaglieri was a long-time critic of the center. In addition, the court said that Battaglieri had failed to show actual malice on the part of the center.

Because false light is very close to libel, the defenses to false light actions are the libel defenses of consent, truth, and qualified privilege.

Public Disclosure of Embarrassing Private Facts

For public disclosure of embarrassing private facts, there needs to be disclosure of such private information that it violates the average person's sensibilities. Private information is defined as information highly offensive to the reasonable person that is not of legitimate public concern.[45] Publication to a broad audience is required for this tort, and newsworthiness is a strong defense.

An example of the public disclosure tort involved an attempt on President Gerald Ford's life and the man who saved him.[46] When Sarah Jane Moore attempted to shoot President Ford in 1975, Oliver Sipple, an ex-marine who happened to be in the crowd that day, deflected the gun and became an instant hero. Sipple was gay, and the gays in California, where he had been living at the time, proudly claimed him as their own. The mainstream media picked up and carried the information of Sipple's sexual orientation. Sipple sued for public disclosure of embarrassing private facts because, although he lived an openly gay lifestyle in California, his family back in the Midwest did not know he was gay. They found out about it in the media and shunned him because of it. The media argued that the fact that Sipple was gay was newsworthy because it helped dispel the image of gays as effeminate, and the court agreed.

Although the newsworthiness defense is strong, it was not successful in one case. Dorothy Barber was hospitalized in Kansas with a rare disease—the more food she consumed, the more weight she lost.[47] A hospital worker notified a freelance photographer of Barber's presence in the hospital. The photographer went to the hospital and took pictures of the emaciated Barber while she slept. The picture appeared in *Time* magazine with the caption, "Insatiable Eater Barber." In the story, she was also referred to as the "Starving Glutton." Barber sued for invasion of privacy for public disclosure of embarrassing private facts. A Missouri trial court agreed with Barber. The photo was not newsworthy, the court held; it was sensationalism, and the average person would be revolted by the picture and caption.

Although public disclosure of private facts usually involves journalists because it requires publication of the information to a broad audience, public relations professionals need to keep the tort in mind when preparing materials involving sensitive issues.

Informational Privacy

In addition to the four torts of privacy is the growing area of informational privacy. Informational privacy is the ability to control information about oneself, and it has become of increasing concern with the growth of the Internet. DoubleClick, an online advertising company, was forced to back down from its publicized decision to match the Web sites someone visited with information gathered offline about that person, such as the person's name and address.[48] And Yahoo! was sued by a man who said he was fired after being identified as the author of critical messages about his bosses. The man claimed Yahoo! released his real name to his employer without his permission.[49]

The success of social networking sites such as MySpace, where middle and high school students post cell phone numbers and other private details on their pages, has added to the concerns about informational privacy. In February 2007, however, a federal court judge ruled that MySpace was not liable for the alleged sexual assault of a 13-year-old girl by a man she met on the site.[50] In a different twist, another victim of a sexual assault sued an ambulance paramedic for invasion of privacy because he posted details about her rape, including where it happened and her description of the assailant, on his MySpace page. The details came from the conversation the woman had with a female police officer in the ambulance on the way to the hospital.[51]

Privacy and Public Relations

Public relations professionals will most often be concerned with appropriation and informational privacy. When photographs of individuals, whether employees or people unconnected with the organization, are taken for use in public relations materials, the consent of the parties involved should be obtained. Usually the consent takes the form of a signed release authorizing the organization to use the person's photograph in promotional materials. Also, an employee should always be asked before information about that employee is used in a newsletter, published in an external publication, or posted on a company Web site. As Frank Walsh put it, "It should not be assumed that a person's status as an employee waives his/her right to privacy."[52]

Care must also be taken in releasing information about employees to the media or other sources. Although the restrictions vary by state and profession, generally the employee information that may be made public without the employee's consent is limited to confirmation of employment, job title, job description, date hired, and date employment terminated.[53]

Causing Personal Injury

Negligence is conduct that falls below the standard established by law for the protection of others against unreasonable risk of harm. The standard established by law is the conduct of a reasonable person acting prudently and with due care under the circumstances. Malpractice is the name most often used for negligence by a professional. Malpractice is defined as professional misconduct or unreasonable lack of skill. Medical malpractice has received the most publicity, but the number of lawsuits against lawyers and accountants is increasing. In malpractice cases, the question is what a reasonable professional, whether a doctor, lawyer, or public relations professional, acting prudently and with due care, would have done in similar circumstances. A person is not liable for injury caused to another by an unavoidable accident or an unintended occurrence that could not be prevented by exercising reasonable care.[54]

A plaintiff in a lawsuit alleging negligence or malpractice must prove four elements:

1. The defendant owed the plaintiff a legal duty of care;
2. The defendant breached that duty of care;
3. The plaintiff was injured as a result of that breach or failure; and
4. The plaintiff was injured.

Duty of Care

Everyone has a duty or an obligation to protect others from harm caused by his or her actions or omissions. The degree of the duty varies with the circumstances, but it is always based on what a reasonable and prudent person would have done in that situation. In malpractice cases, professionals have a duty to act with the same care and skill normally possessed by members of that profession.

Breach of Duty

Once the plaintiff has established that the defendant owed him a duty of care, then the plaintiff must show that the defendant's actions fell short of the reasonable person standard. In other words, the court asks, what would a reasonable person, acting prudently and with due care, have done under the circumstances? If the defendant's behavior was something less than that, a court may consider the defendant to have breached her duty of care to the plaintiff.

Causation

The most important element of negligence is causation. Did the defendant's actions or omissions cause the injury to the plaintiff? The defendant's actions "caused" the injury if they were both the actual and the proximate cause of the injury.

Actual Cause

To determine whether the defendant's actions or omissions were the actual cause of the plaintiff's injury, the courts apply the "but-for" test; that is, the defendant's actions are the actual cause of the plaintiff's injuries if those injuries would not have occurred but for those actions.

Proximate Cause

At the heart of the concept of proximate cause is the notion of foreseeability. Was the result of the defendant's actions or omissions foreseeable? In answering that question, the courts consider:

- the probability that the harm would occur from this action;
- the seriousness of the harm;
- the utility of the conduct creating the harm; and
- the cost of taking precautions to avoid causing the harm.

Palsgraf v. Long Island Railroad Co., a 1928 New York Court of Appeals case, is the landmark case dealing with foreseeability.[55] In the case, Mrs. Palsgraf was standing on a railroad station platform when a train stopped. As it began to depart, one man attempted to jump on board. In helping the man, a train guard on the platform knocked a small package from the man's grasp. The package, which contained fireworks, fell onto the rails and exploded. The shock from the explosion knocked over a scale standing on the other end of the platform, and it landed on Mrs. Palsgraf. She brought an action against the railroad company for her injuries. The court held that her injuries were not foreseeable. The railroad's agents were negligent as to the man they assisted, but there was no way the railroad's agents could have foreseen that the package contained fireworks. As the court put it, "there was nothing in the situation to suggest to the most cautious mind that the parcel wrapped in newspaper would spread wreckage through the station."[56]

Defenses to Negligence

Generally, there are three defenses to negligence: contributory negligence, comparative negligence, and assumption of risk. Contributory negligence occurs when the plaintiff fails to take reasonable care for his own protection. If the plaintiff is found to be contributorily negligent, whether slightly or extensively, she is denied recovery from the defendant. This all-or-nothing aspect of contributory negligence has caused many states to adopt in its stead the doctrine of comparative negligence.

Under comparative negligence, the court divides damages between the parties in proportion to the degree of fault or negligence it finds against them. For example, if Matthew negligently drives his car into Nancy, who is crossing the street against the light, and Nancy sustains damages in the amount of $10,000, a court might determine that Matthew's negligence contributed 70 percent to Nancy's injury and that Nancy's own negligence contributed 30 percent to her injury. Nancy would, then, recover $7,000, or 70 percent of $10,000, from Matthew.

Assumption of risk is the plaintiff's consent to encounter a known danger. A plaintiff who has voluntarily and knowingly assumed the risk of harm arising from the defendant's negligent or reckless conduct cannot recover damages for such harm. For example, football players knowingly assume some risk of injury during the ordinary course of a game when they step onto the football field.

Negligence and Public Relations

Negligence has not been used with any regularity to date against public relations practitioners in the course of their professional duties. That does not mean that the concept of negligence can be ignored, however. Plant tours and open houses, usually planned by public relations departments, can open a company up to liability if a visitor is hurt while on the premises and the company is found to be negligent. Taking precautions in the planning stages of such events can help reduce liability.

In addition, recent cases have suggested a growing willingness on the part of the courts to entertain actions based on negligence where physical harm has resulted from commercial speech. In *Braun v. Soldier of Fortune Magazine, Inc.*, the U.S. Court of Appeals held that *Soldier of Fortune* magazine had a legal duty not to publish an advertisement that subjected the public to a "clearly identifiable unreasonable risk of harm."[57] The action arose when the magazine published an ad reading, "Gun for Hire. . . . All jobs considered." As a result of the ad, Michael Savage, the man who ran the ad, was hired to kill Richard Braun. Savage gunned down Braun and his sixteen-year-old son in front of the family's Atlanta home. The family sued *Soldier of Fortune*, arguing that a reasonably prudent publisher ought to have known that the ad presented a foreseeable risk of unreasonable harm, and the court agreed.

A similar result came in *Weirum v. RKO General*.[58] The radio station RKO had a promotion in which a popular disc jockey would drive from place to place, and teenagers were encouraged to race to the spot to claim prizes. One teenager drove recklessly to get there, killing the driver of another car. The court held that the station was negligent because it was foreseeable that teenagers would drive recklessly to get the prize. This case should serve as notice to public relations professionals to take into consideration the possible behavior of participants when planning promotional activities.

Product Liability

Product liability is the liability of manufacturers and sellers of goods for damages caused by defective products. Product liability can have huge ramifications for a company, not the least of which is monetary. In 1994, a federal district court judge in Birmingham, Alabama, approved a $4.25 billion agreement between Dow Corning Corporation and the women who claimed to have been made ill from its silicone breast implants. The agreement with the makers of the breast implants was the largest product liability settlement in U.S. history and caused Dow Corning to declare bankruptcy one year later. Prior to the 1994 Dow Corning settlement, the largest product liability settlement had been a $3 billion trust established by the Manville Corporation to pay claims stemming from exposure to asbestos.[59]

Besides the pocketbook, companies involved in product liability claims take a direct hit to their reputation. Public relations professionals should be involved in corporate strategic planning to help ease the impact of recalls. Public relations professionals also need to remind companies of their ethical responsibilities to their publics. For example, Ford Motor Company knew that its Pinto car had a gas tank that would not meet new safety standards. Despite that knowledge, Ford decided in 1971 that it was more cost effective to continue producing the Pinto as designed. Between 1971 and 1978, more than 700 people died in accidents involving Pinto fires.[60] Thus, product liability cases involve not only an understanding of the legal issues but also the ethical responsibilities of companies.

The legal liability of manufacturers and sellers of a defective product, or for the product's failure to perform adequately, may be based on a variety of grounds, including negligence. But the most recent and far-reaching development in the field of product liability has been the concept of strict liability. Under strict liability, liability is imposed without regard to fault. The concept was originally developed to deal with situations in which individuals engaged in extremely hazardous activity causing injury to others. Over the years, however, the emphasis has shifted to dangerous products. Under strict liability, sellers are liable for damages that result from selling a product in a defective condition that makes it unreasonably dangerous to the user. The seller is strictly responsible for the damages regardless of whether the seller knew the product was defective. For example, if a glass bottle of cola suddenly exploded in a user's hand, the seller of the cola would be strictly liable for the injuries caused even though the seller might not have acted negligently at all. Liability is imposed by law as a matter of public policy. Nearly all states have adopted some version of strict product liability.

Summary

Public relations professionals must take particular care not to harm others either by damaging their reputation, invading their privacy, or causing them personal injury. Practicing ethical public relations—treating others with respect and dignity—will help reduce the likelihood of harming others through actions or words.

Discussion Questions

1. Ben & Jerry's and The Body Shop are outspoken advocates of environmentally friendly products. Would either be considered limited purpose public figures for the purposes of libel? What factors would you take into consideration in making your determination?

2. You are the vice president of public relations for a large producer of building products. It has recently come to the attention of the company that its siding, installed on about 800,000 homes around the country from 1985 to 1995, warps prematurely, rots in wet weather, and sprouts fungus. The CEO of the company contends that the problems stem from faulty installation, not defective siding. Faced with the threat of lawsuits from angry homeowners, the CEO asks for your advice. What should you advise? What business and ethical issues must you consider before making a decision? What other information would you want before making your decision?

3. Checking out various blogs on the Internet one day, you come across a posting about your boss, the head of a consulting firm. The blogger, another employee, wrote that your boss "is so dull that a 5-watt bulb gives him a run for his money." Keeping an eye on the blog, you discover thirty defamatory statements about your boss and the company in the next few days, all made by the same employee. When you inform your boss, his first reaction is to reach for the phone and call in the attorneys. What should you advise him? Consider whether he might be able to prove the six elements of libel: publication, identification, defamation, fault, falsity, and injury. What category of plaintiff is your boss likely to be? What other factors should you consider in deciding whether to pursue legal action? What strategy might you advise that does not involve legal action?

4. The morning show of radio station KDND staged a "Hold Your Wee for a Wii" contest, promising a free Nintendo video-game system to the listener who could drink the most water without having to relieve himself. A nurse called in to say that the contest was dangerous, but the DJs ignored her warning. It's just water, they contended.

A 28-year-old Sacramento woman drank two gallons of water in an effort to win the Wii and died shortly after of water intoxication. Does the woman's family have a claim against the radio station?

Notes

[1] *Restatement (Second) of Torts* §559 (1977).

[2] Linda Deutsch, "Jury Finds O'Connor Did Not Slander Man Who Gave Son Drugs," *News & Observer*, July 26, 1997, 16A.

[3] 47 U.S.C.S. §230 (Supp. 1996).

[4] *Restatement (Second) of Torts* §564 (1977).

[5] *Nesbitt v. Multimedia, Inc.*, 9 Media L. Rep. (BNA) 1473 (W.D.N.C. 1982).

[6] *Hope v. Hearst Consolidated Publications*, 294 F. 2d 681 (2d Cir. 1961).

[7] *Fawcett Publications, Inc. v. Morris*, 377 P. 2d 42 (Okla.), *appeal dismissed, cert. denied*, 376 U.S. 513 (1962), *reh'g denied*, 377 U.S. 925 (1964).

[8] *Restatement (Second) of Torts* §559(c) (1977).

[9] See *Gazette v. Harris*, 325 S.E. 2d 713 (Va. 1985).

[10] *New York Times v. Sullivan*, 376 U.S. 254 (1964).

[11] *Garrison v. Louisiana*, 379 U.S. 64, 74 (1964); *St. Amant v. Thompson*, 390 U.S. 727, 731 (1968).

[12] *Harte-Hanks Communications, Inc. v. Connaughton*, 491 U.S. 657 (1989).

[13] *Price v. Washington State Senate*, 12 M.L.R. 2035 (1986).

[14] *Hutchinson v. Proxmire*, 443 U.S. 111 (1979); *Franklin v. Lodge 1108*, 97 Cal. App. 3d 915 (Cal. Ct. App. 1979).

[15] *Gertz v. Robert Welch, Inc.*, 418 U.S. 323 (1974).

[16] *Carson v. Allied News Co.*, 529 F. 2d 206 (7th Cir. 1976); *Buckley v. Littell*, 539 F. 2d 882 (2d Cir. 1976), *cert. denied*, 429 U.S. 1062 (1977); *Reliance Insurance Co. v. Barron's*, 442 F. Supp. 1341 (S.D.N.Y. 1977).

[17] *Wilson v. Daily Gazette*, 588 S.E. 2d 197, 208 (W. Va. 2003).

[18] *Wolston v. Reader's Digest Ass'n*, 443 U.S. 157 (1979).

[19] *Hutchinson v. Proxmire*, 443 U.S. (1979).

[20] *Bieter v. Fetzer*, 2005 Minn. App. LEXIS 24.

[21] *Yiamouyiannis v. Consumers Union of United States*, 619 F. 2d 932 (2d Cir. 1980); *Cloyd v. Press, Inc.*, 629 S.W. 2d 24 (Tenn. App. 1981); *Liberty Lobby, Inc. v. Anderson*, 562 F. Supp. 201 (D.D.C. 1983), *aff'd*, 746 F. 2d 1563 (D.C. Cir. 1984), *vacated on other grds*, 477 U.S. 242 (1986).

[22] *Vegod Corp. v. ABC*, 603 P. 2d 14 (Cal. 1980).

[23] *Steaks Unlimited, Inc. v. Deaner*, 468 F. Supp. 779 (W.D. Pa. 1979), *aff'd*, 623 F. 2d 264 (3d Cir. 1980).

[24] *New York in Chapadeau v. Utica Observer-Dispatch, Inc.*, 341 N.E. 2d 569, 1 Media L. Rep. (BNA) 1693 (N.Y. 1975).

[25] *Philadelphia Newspapers v. Hepps*, 475 U.S. 767 (1986).

[26] *Dun & Bradstreet, Inc. v. Greenmoss Builders, Inc.*, 472 U.S. 749 (1985).

[27] *Gertz v. Welch*.

[28] Ibid., at 339.

[29] *Milkovich v. Lorain Journal Co.*, 497 U.S. 1 (1990).

[30] *Unelko v. Rooney*, 912 F. 2d 1049 (1990).

[31] *Hustler Magazine, Inc. v. Falwell*, 485 U.S. 46 (1988).

[32] *Tech Plus, Inc. v. Ansel*, 793 N.E. 2d 1256 (Mass. Ct. App. 2003), *review denied*, 799 N.E. 2d 594 (Mass. 2003).

[33] "Farmers Refuse to Take the Fall for Taco Bell," *Bulldog Reporter*, March 24, 2007, http://www.bulldogreporter.com/dailydog/issues/1_1/dailydog_pr_biz_update/6794-1.html?type=pf (accessed March 26, 2007).

[34] *Garziano v. E. I. DuPont de Nemours and Co.*, 818 F. 2d 380 (5th Cir. 1987).

[35] Keith Ecker, "Trash Talk," *InsideCounsel* (October 2006): 42.

[36] Louis Brandeis and Samuel Warren, "The Right to Privacy," *Harvard Law Review* 4 (1890): 220.

[37] William Prosser, "Privacy," *California Law Review* 48 (1960): 383–423.

[38] *Le Mistral v. CBS*, 402 N.Y.S. 2d 815 (1978).

[39] *Zacchini v. Scripps Howard Broadcasting Co.*, 433 U.S. 562 (1977).

[40] *Carson v. Here's Johnny Portable Toilets, Inc.*, 698 F. 2d 831 (1983).

[41] *Midler v. Young & Rubicam*, 944 F. 2d 909 (9th Cir. 1991), *cert. denied*, 503 U.S. 951 (1992).

[42] *Battaglieri v. Mackinac Center for Public Policy*, 261 Mich. App. 296, 680 N.W. 2d 915, 2004 Mich. App. LEXIS 759 (Mich. Ct. App. 2004).

[43] Ibid., 298–299.

[44] *Time, Inc. v. Hill*, 385 U.S. 374 (1967).

[45] *Restatement (Second) of Torts* (1977).

[46] *Sipple v. Chronicle Publishing Co.*, 201 Cal. Rptr. 665 (Cal. Ct. App. 1984).

[47] *Barber v. Time, Inc.* 159 S.W. 2d 291 (1942).

[48] A. Petersen, "A Privacy Firestorm at DoubleClick," *Wall Street Journal*, February 23, 2000, B1.

[49] R. Kerber, "Lawsuit to Test Online Free Speech Rights," *Tuscaloosa News*, May 14, 2000, D1.

[50] Dawn C. Chmielewski and Jim Puzzanghera, "Judge Says MySpace isn't Liable for Alleged Sexual Assault on Girl," *Los Angeles Times*, February 15, 2007, C1.

[51] Maxine Bernstein, "Rape Victim Sues Over MySpace Post," *Oregonian*, April 28, 2007, E01.

[52] F. Walsh, *Public Relations and the Law* (New York: Foundation for Public Relations Education and Research, 1988), 15.

[53] David Guth and Charles Marsh, *Public Relations: A Values-Driven Approach* (Boston: Allyn & Bacon, 2000).

[54] Richard A. Mann and Barry S. Roberts, *Contemporary Business Law* (Minneapolis: West, 1996).

[55] *Palsgraf v. Long Island Railroad Co.*, 248 N.Y. 339 (N.Y. Ct. App. 1928).

[56] Ibid., 345.

[57] *Braun v. Soldier of Fortune Magazine, Inc.*, 968 F. 2d 1110, 20 Media L. Rep. (BNA) 1777 (11th Cir. 1992), *cert. denied*, 113 S. Ct. 1028 (1993).

[58] *Weirum v. RKO General*, 539 P. 2d 36 (1975).

[59] "$4.2 Billion Implant Settlement Approved," *New York Times*, September 2, 1994.

[60] William Shaw and Vincent Barry, *Moral Issues in Business*, 6th ed. (Belmont, CA: Wadsworth, 1995).

chapter five

PROTECTING CREATIVE PROPERTY

Intellectual property is the legal name given to such intangible property as copyrights, trademarks, and patents. Protection of intellectual property is provided for in the U.S. Constitution. Congress is specifically given the power "[t]o promote the Progress of Science and useful Arts, by securing for limited Times to Authors and Inventors the exclusive Right to their respective Writings and Discoveries."[1] Essentially, Congress is given the right to grant time-limited monopolies to owners of intellectual property.

Protecting Creative Expression: Copyright

Copyright is a form of protection given to "original works of authorship in any tangible medium of expression, now known or later developed" and is governed by the federal Copyright Act.[2] The purpose of copyright is to encourage artistic expression.

Original Works

The term "original works" includes:

- Literary, musical, and dramatic works
- Pantomimes and choreographic works
- Pictorial, graphic, and sculptural works
- Motion picture and other audiovisual works
- Sound recordings
- Architectural works

The concept of "original works" entails some minimum amount of creativity. The U.S. Supreme Court has held, for example, that the alphabetical arrangement of names in a telephone book does not constitute sufficient creativity or originality for copyright protection.[3] Feist Publications had sought permission from Rural Telephone Service Co. to use the information contained in Rural's white pages telephone directory. Feist intended to publish a directory covering a larger geographic area than that contained in Rural's directory. Rural refused to grant permission, but Feist proceeded to copy much of Rural's directory anyway. Rural sued Feist for copyright infringement. The Supreme Court said that Rural's directory enjoyed no copyright protection because it contained no originality. The directory merely was an alphabetical listing of names and telephone numbers.

Because copyright is meant to protect creativity and originality, facts are not subject to copyright protection. In *Feist*, the facts in the directory—names and telephone numbers—were not the issue. At issue was the copying of the arrangement and selection of the names and numbers. Similarly, copyright does not protect ideas, only the expression of ideas. If "A" tells "B" the great story idea she has, and "B" takes that idea and turns it into a best-selling book, "A" has no recourse against "B" under copyright law. "B's" actions may be unethical, but he did not violate any copyright laws.

Protection of the expression of an idea begins as soon as the work is fixed in a tangible medium. Disks, CDs, and Web sites are considered fixed for purposes of copyright. Prior to 1978, copyright protection did not begin until the work was registered with the Copyright Office. Registration is not required for works created post-1978, although it is recommended because certain legal remedies for infringement depend on registration.

Ownership

Copyright belongs initially to the author or joint authors of the original work. Usually the author is the one who creates the work. But there are two times under the doctrine of work-made-for-hire when this is not the case: when a work is made during the regular course of employment and when it is contracted to be made. Computer programmers employed by Microsoft, for example, do not own the copyright to the software they develop during the course of their employment; Microsoft is considered the author and owner of the copyright. Similarly, if a company commissions or orders a work for a special purpose, the company and the creator of the work may contract that the company will own the work for purposes of copyright.

It should be noted, however, that most freelance photographers and public relations firms retain ownership of the copyright of their work. Permission to use the work in ways other than that originally contracted for must be obtained from the owner. Permission to use photographs or materials in printed publications does not extend automatically to online publications. Ownership of a copyright may be transferred, but the transfer must be in writing and signed by the owner or authorized agent of the owner.

Owner's Rights

The Copyright Act gives the copyright owner the exclusive right to:

- Reproduce the work
- Prepare derivative works based on the work
- Distribute copies or recordings of the work
- Perform the work publicly
- Display the work publicly

Since 1990, the copyright owner also has limited moral rights. Moral rights apply only to original works of art, sculpture, and other works of visual arts that are produced in 200 copies or fewer. Moral rights were added to bring American copyright law more into line with international copyright. Moral rights grant to the artist the right to have his or her name kept on the work or to have the artist's name removed from it if the work has been altered in a way that is objectionable to the artist. Moral rights also give artists limited rights to prevent their works from being defaced or destroyed. Essentially, these rights recognize the special connection between artists and their work. It ensures the integrity of the work as art is maintained. The City of Indianapolis, for example, violated the moral rights of a sculptor when the city demolished his large, metal work that had been installed on city property.[4]

Duration of the Protection

For works created after 1978, copyright protection lasts for the life of the author plus seventy years. A copyright owned by a

corporation lasts for ninety-five years from the date of publication or 120 years from the date of creation, whichever is shorter.[5]
Works created before 1978 vary in the length of the protection
depending on whether and when the works were published.

After the expiry of the copyright term, the work enters the
public domain and may be used freely by anyone. Works created
before 1923 are now in the public domain. Works produced by
the federal government are not subject to copyright and are
always in the public domain.

Infringement of Owner's Rights

Infringement of copyright occurs whenever somebody exer-
cises without consent one of the copyright owner's rights.
Infringement need not be intentional. To prove infringement, the
plaintiff need merely prove ownership and that the defendant
infringed one of the rights. Although, as indicated earlier, registration of the copyright is no longer required under U.S. law, registration of the work with the Copyright Office is required before
a plaintiff can sue for copyright infringement. Whether the work
is registered, the copyright notice ©, plus the date and the
owner's name should be affixed to all publicly distributed copies
of the work to serve as notice to all users that the work is under
copyright. If proper notice appears on all copies, defendants cannot mitigate damages by claiming they did not know the work
was protected by copyright. It should also be noted that copyright applies to the Internet. Copying or downloading images or
text from a Web site may well be an infringement of copyright.
To avoid infringing copyright laws, permission to use another's
work should always be obtained.

Remedies for infringement include an injunction, impound-
ment and possible destruction of the articles, actual damages
plus any profits made by the defendant, and costs of the lawsuit.

Limitations on Owner's Rights

Although the copyright owner is entitled to exclusive rights
with respect to the work, those rights are subject to several limitations.

Compulsory Licensing

Compulsory licensing permits certain limited uses of copyrighted material on the payment of royalties and compliance
with statutory conditions.

First-Sale Doctrine

Under section 109(a) of the Copyright Act, once the owner of a copyright authorizes the release of lawfully made copies, those copies may in turn be passed along to others by sale, rental, and loan. But ownership of a copyright is distinct from ownership of the physical work itself. Therefore, the purchase of a textbook does not affect the publisher's copyright. Nor does it authorize the purchaser to make and sell copies of the book or create derivative works from it.

Fair Use

The Copyright Act provides that the fair use of copyrighted material for purposes such as criticism, comment, news reporting, teaching, scholarship, or research is not an infringement of copyright. In determining whether the use is fair, the courts consider four factors:

- the purpose and character of the use, including whether the use is of a commercial nature or is for nonprofit educational purposes;
- the nature of the work;
- the amount and substantiality of the portion of the work used; and
- the effect of the use on the potential market value of the work.

There are no quick answers with fair use, but some general guidelines should be kept in mind:

- If only a small part of a work is used, the more likely it is that the use will be considered fair.
- The use will more likely be considered fair if its purpose is for news reporting, critical commentary, or parody.
- Commercial copying is generally considered unfair. In the eyes of the courts, commercial means making money from the copying; it does not matter whether the copying is done by a not-for-profit or a for-profit organization. In both cases, it is commercial copying.

Downloading music from a site such as Kazaa, even on a "try-before-you-buy" basis, is a copyright infringement and is not a fair use.[6] Similarly, posting video clips from TV shows to the Web site YouTube is an infringement. Google's Book Search site is currently testing the limits of fair use. Google has digitized thousands of books, many of which are still under copyright. It lets users see the full text of books in the public domain. If the book is still under copyright, however, the user can search the book, but Google only displays short segments of the text that surround the search terms. Google argues that because users have access only to short segments of the book, it is fair use. Many writers and publishers, however, claim that Google has violated their copyright by digitizing the whole work in the first place, regardless of how much access it gives subsequently to users.[7]

Protecting Goodwill: Trademark

Trademark law governs the use of brand names and other words or symbols associated with a product or service. Its purpose is to facilitate consumers' purchase decisions by allowing them to identify the quality and dependability of a product or service with a trademark.[8] It also protects against competitors taking advantage of a company's good name and reputation and depriving it of business. Thus, trademark can be seen as protecting the goodwill or reputation of a company. The Federal Trademark Act (the Lanham Act) prohibits businesses from using someone else's mark in connection with any goods or services. The act also prevents a business from falsely describing or representing its own goods and services. In 1988, Congress amended the act to prohibit the misrepresentation of another person's goods, services, or commercial activities.[9]

A trademark serves to identify tangible products. A service mark, on the other hand, is used to identify and distinguish the services of one person from those of another. A trade or service mark can be any word, symbol, design, or color, provided it meets three criteria:

1. It must be in use as an identifier of the product.
2. It must be distinctive. It cannot be ordinary, merely descriptive, or generic. If, however, a descriptive word becomes so linked with the goods or service so as to be inseparable from them, then it can be distinctive and serve as a mark. Conversely, if a trademark loses its distinctiveness and becomes simply descriptive, it loses protection. Nylon, thermos, aspirin, and cellophane are examples of trademarks that lost protection because they became generic. A line of clothing has been held not to be

distinctive enough to qualify for trademark protection. Samara Bros., a children's clothing designer, sued Wal-Mart Stores for reproducing its lines of clothing, claiming that in copying the design of the clothes, Wal-Mart had infringed its trademark. The Supreme Court rejected the argument that a line of clothing, without something more, could be distinctive for the purposes of trademark.[10]

3. It must not be confusingly similar to someone else's trademark. Marks are confusingly similar when reasonable people would be confused by the marks; that is, they would associate the two goods together when they have no connection with each other. The same word can be used as two different marks provided a reasonable person would not assume an association. For example, Mead Data Central sued Toyota over Toyota's use of the word Lexus for its car line.[11] Mead Data argued that Lexus was so similar to its own legal database service called Lexis that consumers would be confused. Toyota argued in return that consumers did not confuse Lotus computer software with Lotus cars. The courts agreed with Toyota—a reasonable consumer would not be confused.

As with copyright, there is no registration requirement for trademark protection. Once a logo is used on an organization's letterhead, for example, the logo is a trademark. But also as in the case of copyright, there are certain advantages to registering the mark. Registration is evidence of the first use of the trademark by the company, it permits the owner to sue in federal court for infringement, and the registration symbol ® serves as notice to others of a claim of ownership. If the trademark is not registered, the owner may use the symbol ™ or ℠.

Registration of a trademark lasts ten years but can be renewed indefinitely. Trademark rights can be lost only through abandonment, dilution, or infringement. Trademark rights are abandoned if the mark's use is discontinued with an intent not to resume its use. Dilution occurs when the mark is permitted to be used as a generic term, meaning that many people have infringed the trademark rights by using the mark. As a result, the mark loses its distinctiveness and its rights.

Actions arise for trademark infringement when someone uses "in commerce any reproduction, counterfeit, copy, or colorable imitation of a registered mark in connection with the sale, offering for sale, distribution, or advertising of any goods or services" without the owner's consent.[12] The question of whether Internet keyword searches constitutes the use of a mark "in commerce" has recently come before the courts. The search engine Google, through its AdWords, allows advertisers to buy keywords. When a search engine user enters those keywords, the advertiser's link appears at the top of the search results page as a "sponsored link." Google allows advertisers to buy someone else's trademark as a keyword. For example, the online realty company, TheMLSonline.com, purchased the Edina Realty trademark as a keyword.[13] Thus, when someone typed in Edina Realty, the search results page showed TheMLSonline.com link at the top. The courts are divided on whether that constitutes a "use in commerce" and is, therefore, actionable under the Lanham Act. Until the matter is settled, advertisers should be careful about buying a competitor's trademark as a keyword. Advertisers would be wise to choose more generic, descriptive keywords to minimize their risk of liability.

Once the use of the mark is held to constitute a use in commerce, the question becomes whether the use is likely to cause confusion among consumers. In deciding whether there is a likelihood of confusion, courts consider the following factors:

- the degree of similarity between the owner's mark and the infringing mark;
- the strength of the owner's mark;
- the degree of care exercised by the consumers;
- the length of time the defendant has used the mark without evidence of actual confusion;
- the intent of the defendant in adopting the mark;
- the evidence of actual confusion;
- the channels of trade and advertising of the goods or services;
- the relatedness or proximity of the two companies' products or services; and
- the likelihood of expansion in product lines.[14]

For example, Pizzeria Uno Corporation sued a restaurant owner for infringement for opening a Taco Uno restaurant.[15] The Lanham Act provides protection against misuse or infringement by injunctive relief, where the court enjoins or orders the company to stop using the name, and a right of action for damages.

In 1996, Congress passed the Federal Trademark Dilution Act to protect well-known marks from dilution.[16] Dilution occurs when the mark is used in a way that causes it to lose its distinctiveness or disparages it. For example, the lingerie manufacturer, Victoria's Secret, asked the owners of a Kentucky "adult novelties" store to change its name from Victor's Secret on the basis that the name infringed the more famous trademark. When the owners changed it to Victor's Little Secret, Victoria's Secret sued for dilution, arguing that the store's name disparaged Victoria's Secret. The Supreme Court found in 2003 that there was "a complete absence of evidence of any lessening of the capacity of the Victoria's Secret mark to identify . . . goods . . . sold in Victoria's Secret stores or advertised in its catalogs."[17] In other words, Victoria's Secret was not able to show that there was actual dilution of its mark caused by the existence of Victor's Little Secret.

Many companies work hard to protect their rights from infringement and dilution. To those who do not understand trademark law, the actions of these companies often appear overly aggressive. Public relations professionals need to be aware of this potential for backlash.

For example, Pinehurst, Inc., owners of the Pinehurst Country Club in the Village of Pinehurst, North Carolina, had to apologize for forcing a number of village businesses to drop "Pinehurst" from their names.[18] Pinehurst, Inc., has a federally registered trademark on the use of the word "Pinehurst" but angered many villagers when it said the name belonged to the company, not the village. In a full-page ad in the local newspaper, the company wrote, "Unfortunately, we were overzealous, we made some mistakes, and we did not communicate as well as we should have."

Public relations professionals, then, can play a key role in educating the public on the proper use of a trademark and on why the company may need to be aggressive in defending that use.

Protecting Inventions: Patents

Patent law applies to inventions and is governed by the same provision of the Constitution as copyright protection. Although most public relations practitioners will not deal with patents unless they work in a pharmaceutical or research-oriented industry, it is important to understand the differences among copyright, trademark, and patent law. All three comprise the law of intellectual property and protect different aspects of it. Copyright grants a monopoly over the expression of ideas; trademark protects the good name of a company; and patent law grants a monopoly over inventions.

A patent grants an inventor the right to make, use, or sell an invention to the exclusion of all others for a period of twenty years from the date of application. Once the patent expires, the invention enters the public domain, and anyone may use it.

Inventions that may be patented include any process, machine, manufacture, composition of matter, or any improvement on those. To qualify for a patent, an invention must meet three conditions:

- **Utility.** It must be useful.
- **Novelty.** It must be new.
- **Nonobviousness.** It cannot simply be a reworking of an existing invention in such a way that anyone else could duplicate it.

Summary

A valuable asset of a company is its creative property. Creative property, whether the expression of ideas, goodwill, or an invention is protected by federal legislation. The owners of creative property are granted exclusive rights to determine the use of that property. Public relations professionals need to protect their clients' rights as well as avoid infringing the creative property rights of others.

	Copyright	Trademark	Patent
What is protected?	Expression of ideas	Goodwill or reputation	Invention
Rights protected	Reproduce, prepare derivative works, distribute, perform, display	Use or sell	Make, use, or sell
Length of time	Generally, life of author plus 70 years	Until abandoned	20 years from date of application
Requirements for protection	Original and fixed	Distinctive and in use	Novel, useful, and nonobvious

Discussion Questions

1. As part of your job for Y Corporation, you scan newspapers and trade publications for mention of the company. When you see a reference, you clip the article, photocopy it, and circulate it among the managers. Are you infringing the copyright of the publications? If so, could you use fair use as a defense?

2. In preparing a new brochure for Y Corporation, you discover an old photograph taken by a freelance photographer. The photo had been used originally in an annual report several years ago, but it fits perfectly with your theme for the new brochure. Your supervisor tells you to use it because, after all, the company paid for the shot. What is your response?

3. Tiny Tots Day Care is suddenly using a teddy bear in its ads that looks remarkably like Y Corporation's trademarked teddy bear. Legal counsel wants to send a cease-and-desist letter to the day-care provider telling it to immediately stop using the character. Y Corporation has had some negative press recently for being heavy handed in dealing with employees. You are afraid that if the media got wind of the attorney's letter, Y Corporation would look even worse. What might you advise the company to do and why?

Notes

[1] U.S. Const., art. 1, § 8.

[2] 17 U.S.C. §101.

[3] *Feist Publications, Inc. v. Rural Telephone Service Co., Inc.*, 499 U.S. 340 (1991).

[4] *Martin v. Indianapolis*, 982 F. Supp. 625 (1997), 4 F. Supp. 2d 808 (S.D. Ind., 1998).

[5] Term Extension Act, PL. 105-298.

[6] *BMG Music v. Gonzalez*, 430 F. 3d 888, 2005 U.S. App. LEXIS 26903 (7th Cir. 2005).

[7] Steve Seidenberg, "Copyright Clash," *Inside Counsel* (November 2006): 22.

[8] Jonathan L. Schwartz, "Making the Consumer Watchdog's Bark as Strong as its Gripe," *Albany Law Journal of Science and Technology* 16 (2006): 59.

[9] Trademark Law Revision Act, Pub. L. No. 100-667, 102 Stat. 3935 (1988).

[10] *Wal-Mart Stores, Inc. v. Samara Bros.*, 529 U.S. 205 (2000).

[11] *Mead Data Central, Inc. v. Toyota Motor Sales, U.S.A., Inc.*, 875 F. 2d 1026, 10 U.S.P.Q. 2d 1961 (2nd Cir. 1989).

[12] Lanham Act, 15 U.S.C. § 1114(1)(a)

[13] *Edina Realty v. TheMLSonline.com*, 2006 WL 737064 (D. Minn. 2006).

[14] *Checkpoint Systems, Inc. v. Check Point Software Technologies, Inc.*, 104 F. Supp. 2d 427, 456-7 (D. N.J. 2000) (citing *Fisons Horticulture, Inc. v. Vigoro Industries, Inc.*, 30 F. 3d 466, 473 (3rd Cir. 1994)); *AMF, Inc. v. Sleekcraft Boats*, 599 F. 2d 341, 348 n. 11 (9th Cir. 1979).

[15] *Pizzeria Uno Corporation v. Temple*, 747 F. 2d 1522 (1984).

[16] Federal Trademark Dilution Act, 15 U.S.C. §§ 1125(c), 1127.

[17] *Moseley v. V Secret Catalogue, Inc.*, 537 U.S. 418. 434 (2003).

[18] Editorial, "Pinehurst is Pinehurst; Forget about Pinehurst," *News & Record*, August 1, 1999, H2.

INDEX